BATTLE READY

BATTLE READY

MARK R. LITTLETON

VICTOR BOOKS®

A DIVISION OF SCRIPTURE PRESS PUBLICATIONS INC.
USA CANADA ENGLAND

All Scripture references are from the *Holy Bible, New International Version,* © 1973, 1978, 1984, International Bible Society. Used by permission of Zondervan Bible Publishers.

Copyediting: Michael Kendrick and Barbara Williams

Cover Design: Joe DeLeon

Cover Illustration: Tony Mujica

Library of Congress Cataloging-in-Publication Data

Littleton, Mark R., 1950-
  Battle ready / Mark R. Littleton.
    p.   cm.
  Includes bibliographical references.
  ISBN 0-89693-577-9
  1. Temptation. 2. Devil. I. Title.
BT725.L57   1992
241'.3–dc20   91-30778
                                                             CIP

---

1 2 3 4 5 6 7 8 9 10 Printing/Year 96 95 94 93 92

CONTENTS

DEDICATION

To Aunt Beth and Uncle Harry
Aunt Connie and Uncle Holland

Family afar but near at heart

SIN, SIN, EVERYWHERE, AND EVERY DROP CAN SINK

INTRODUCTION

As 1990 drew to a close, many newspapers and magazines offered a brief year in review. Consider some of the world's great and not-so-great moments:

General Manuel Noriega surrendered to U.S. forces on January 3, after years of shoveling drugs into the U.S.

On February 15, Colombia sponsored a "Drug Summit." President Bush attended. World leaders forged plans to stop the flow of cocaine from Colombia to countless nations.

Thieves crept into a Boston gallery and heisted numerous priceless works of art on March 18.

On March 22, the captain of the oil freighter *Exxon Valdez*, Joseph Hazelwood, was convicted of being drunk while commanding his ship. The oil spill caused by the ship's accident continues to trouble the waters of Alaska.

Eighty-seven people died in an arson fire March 25 in the Bronx.

On April 7, John Poindexter, convicted of conspiracy in the Iran-Contra scam, received a six-month prison sentence.

April 24: Michael Milken pleaded guilty to making fraudulent deals on Wall Street. In previous years he made nearly a half billion dollars through his schemes.

A patient suffering from Alzheimer's disease used a "suicide machine" to kill herself on June 5.

The President's son, Neil Bush, was accused on July 5 of "conflict of interest" by serving as a member of the Silverado Bank's board. Later, regulators filed a $200 million lawsuit against Silverado.

Pete Rose, one of baseball's greats, was sentenced on July 19 to five months in prison. Why? Tax evasion.

Iraqi troops overran Kuwait and took over the government on August 2.

Marion Barry, mayor of Washington, D.C., was convicted on charges of cocaine possession on August 10. He was sentenced to six months in prison.

On August 26, the first of five victims of a serial murderer was discovered in Gainesville, Florida.

Businessman Charles Keating was formally charged with a junk bond swindle on September 19. Later, five senators, including former astronaut John Glenn, were accused of violating Senate ethics rules.

The possibility of war in the Middle East escalated as President Bush doubled the number of American troops stationed there on November 8.

On December 14 a Missouri judge allowed Nancy Cruzan's feeding tube to be removed after she had been in a coma for eight years. Twelve days later, she died.[1]

What a year for . . . temptation!

Absolutely. What are most of these events but the results of sin that began with a temptation long before the event occurred? The temptation in the Garden of Eden launched us into a world filled with evil. If there is a number-one culprit for all the devastation we see, it's temptation. The devil, our fleshly natures, and the world spur us on to acts we later regret, confess, commiserate over, and bemoan for years afterward. Sin starts with temptation. Temptation begins with a suggestion, planted by ourselves or our personal tempter,

[1]Information taken from "1990: The Year in Review," *The Washington Times*, December 31, 1990, p. A5.

whether he be human or demonic.

Conquering this grave problem, though, is more than learning and practicing a few simple rules. We have all the rules before us. It's practicing the rules and living by truth that get us down. We fail, flub up, "make a mistake," think "irrationally," "commit an error," "blow it," "go to pot," misbehave, stray, lapse, trip, break the law, go wrong, "commit a sin," "fall from grace," go astray, transgress, trespass, offend, "slip up," "lose it." We have a million ways to make the excuse. Actually, the problem is sin we can't overcome on our own.

I believe that apart from Jesus Christ, there is no hope for anyone who wants to reform his inner self. Only He can change the heart. Only He can create the new nature within us that will enable us to live godly, decent, loving, and moral lives. In this world we'll never be sinless. But while a Christian isn't sinless, he should be sinning less and less.

How do you arrive at that point? How do you begin to overcome temptation?

This book will help you on that road. Some of the answers will surprise you. But I hope you will join me in life's greatest adventure: gaining victory through hard, rational, Spirit-guided choices. Victory is indeed a choice. Making the right choices is what this book hopes to help you do.

BATTLE CRY!

WE'RE IN A WAR

CHAPTER 1

Perhaps it was idle curiosity.

No, on the contrary, now I realize the whole process crawled, then meandered, then eventually galloped yard by yard. It was executed like a Joe Montana touchdown drive. A master strategist, skilled in the art of battle, devised the plan and rattled off the orders as surely and confidently as Wellington at Waterloo.

It started harmlessly enough. A novel. I wanted to read a "major" novel. I hadn't read a "secular" novel of any sort since becoming a Christian in 1972. Frankly, I feared them. I didn't want to corrupt my mind. But some new inner notion nudged me that winter of 1976. I said to myself, "You really should know something about what's being published." I queried Mom. She suggested Herman Wouk. While in college during the '60s I'd read *The Caine Mutiny*. I picked up a copy of *The Winds of War*. It was fascinating, riveting. The dialogue gripped me. The plot was spellbinding. The characters seemed to come to life. I read with passion, even awe. I couldn't put it down.

Afterward, I thought, "Well, I've done it. I know what's being published. That's enough." It was a good read, a joyful read, and one I felt absolutely no sense of remorse or guilt about. Why should I? There was nothing immoral, sinister, evil, or depraved about it. The book offered fascinating entertainment, a few hours of relaxation and escape, and some stark and vivid insights. I would read it again today.

In 1980, though, I happened to read *Time's* "Ten Best Books of the Decade." The critic listed among them William Styron's *Sophie's Choice*. I thought again, "If it's that good, maybe I ought to check it out.

I was appalled from the start by the book's graphic sex scenes. But I kept telling myself this was art and I should endure it, if only to be able to converse intelligently with non-Christians. I soon found, though, that any conversation into which I introduced the question, "Oh, have you read *Sophie's Choice*?" quickly sped through, "Did you like it?" and "I thought it was good" and then to a wholly different topic. Undaunted, I told myself I'd reaped some benefit from it, though I couldn't quite put my finger on what it was.

Years passed. Now and then I read a new offering. I found some of Taylor Caldwell's books interesting, discovered new authors like Chaim Potok, Walker Percy, and Tom Clancy, and began picking other Christians' minds about who wrote a good novel, even if it wasn't particularly Christian. Naturally, I also enjoyed some of the Christian authors who spun out new tales of war and woe.

But because I aspired to become a novelist, I had to know what made a best-seller. Something inside me urged, "You need to read the best. Go for it."

My mother-in-law commented on one I picked by Erskine Caldwell, *God's Little Acre:* "Isn't that kind of — uh — risqué?" I responded, "It's a classic." She said, "It's a classic because it was the first mainstream novel that got away with graphic sex." I swallowed and decided not to read any more. She knew too much.

But I moved on to others. I tried about twenty pages of Judith Krantz and came away disgusted. But also fascinated. Soon, I found myself reading some of the "big sexy novelists" — Danielle Steel, Harold Robbins, Sidney Sheldon. I told myself it was all right, I could deal with it, there was no problem. My wife didn't like it, but I explained to her that I needed to find out how authors put together successful novels.

Then in the middle of a new offering I noticed something strange had occurred. I began skipping pages, reading quickly over the narrative, and hitting only the sexy parts. I didn't care about the story or the characters. I just wanted the red hot sex. I put the book down and asked myself, "What's the next stop — adultery?"

I loaded up my wagon, took the haul back to the library, and resolved not to read another piece of fiction unless I knew for certain that it had genuine moral and spiritual value.

THE SLIDE

I've taken these few paragraphs to illustrate something I've seen over and over, both in my life and others': the slow but steady progress of temptation. C.S. Lewis once wrote that Satan doesn't much care how he gets you — murder, cards, gossip — it really doesn't matter. His goal is moving us away from God. The devil works millimeter by millimeter over years at a time to move us away from faith, commitment, and growth. He's the master tinkerer. He loves to plink and tick and scrape away at us, nailing bad habits in place until he has a completely worldly and worthless Christian.

I'm not saying that reading novels or contemporary fiction is wrong, though I'm convinced there's very little out there with true "artistic" value, let alone something of spiritual uplift. But the temptation I experienced with worldly novels happens to others with drinking, entertainment, anger, discipline, envy, love of money. As a child of the '60s, I excoriated my parents for what I perceived as their rank materialism. But what do I worry and fret about more than anything now in my existence? Money. Maybe Mom and Dad weren't such pagans after all!

The list in Galatians 5:19-21 describes "immorality, impurity, sensuality, idolatry, sorcery" — those temptations that come at us in legions. You can't pass a modern billboard without it blasting a hole in your attempts at sanctification. You can't watch a video today without being pelted with indecency of some sort.

On top of all this, the world screams in our faces, "It's art. It's entertainment. It's just fun. You Christians are a bunch of prudes!" Remarks like that get our hackles up. "Prude? PRUDE! I'll show them! I'll ... I'll...."

In my secular writer's group one night, a friend wrote a rather funny but vulgar line. I laughed. (I know I wasn't supposed to, but it came out before I had a chance to do anything about it.) I commented that the line was funny, but I wouldn't repeat it to anyone. Immediately, one of the other members, knowing that I was a Christian, remarked, "What's the matter, Mark? You can laugh at it, but you won't say the word?"

Have you ever felt like cutting loose with a series of obscenities? Have you ever wanted to forget the whole Christian trip and spend a night on The Block (Baltimore's red-light district)?

If Satan can't trick you, he'll trap you. If he can't trap you, he'll slap you. This world at times seems like nothing less than a personal boxing match in which we face Mike Tyson in the morning, Sugar Ray Leonard at lunch, Marvelous Marvin Hagler before dinner, and Evander Holyfield at bedtime. I know—no one can lay a glove or a fiery dart on us unless God allows it, right? But if you ask me, He lets an awful lot get through!

I suppose it's funny. We can always laugh at our pain—afterward. But if there's anything I've discovered about temptation it's that it never gets easier, it never lets up, and it never loses ground on one front without starting something new on another.

We're in a war. It's true Jesus has won that war. But it doesn't always feel like that down here on the front lines. It's also true that God has outfitted us with marvelous fighting gear and sure commands for victory. But frequently it seems (I know it's only my imagination, but ... it still *seems*) like nothing works, nothing will work, and the Bible's promises do little more than mock me and pile on the guilt.

Is it possible to win over temptation?

Yes.

But let me qualify that. I believe some temptations never get off the pavement; they simply aren't that interesting.

Others strike during certain periods in our lives. We fight back in the Spirit and win. They don't return for a second bout. Still other temptations strike us seasonally. We fight them off, think they're down and out, but lo, they burst out again at the same time next year. Before we know it, we're hit. We get up and fight back. It goes away, only to explode again at the wrong moment.

Then there are the temptations that fell us time after time. We memorize Scripture. We keep "in the Word." We get involved in church. We pray. We get others praying. And still temptations defeat us.

Why? Is it because we're weak? Certainly. Is it because we haven't done enough? Possibly. Is it because we really haven't faced the fact that it's sin? Perhaps. Is it because we haven't gotten down to the root of the issue? Undoubtedly.

Yet, just knowing why we give in to sin isn't enough. The problem I face is temptation that keeps coming back, and back, and back. And I keep giving in, and in, and in.

I've tried to understand why certain temptations in my life seem so difficult. Why has rock music had such a hold on me? Even though I'm selective in whom I listen to, I can find something delicious and sublime in some of the worst music. I constantly struggle to avoid listening to certain musicians I know are ungodly.

Discipline! Good grief. The battle begins every morning. Just getting up on days I don't have a defined schedule has never been easy. I read recently how a famous author goes to bed at 1 A.M. and gets up at 5 A.M., totally refreshed, full of energy? Why can't I be like that—even after seven or eight hours in the sack?

And lust! Please understand. I'm not a sex maniac. I've never committed adultery, rape, or indulged in pornography (in my born again days). But just a walk through the mall can devastate me. Every woman begins to look seductive.

What's to be done? In eighteen years as a Christian, few of the temptations have changed. Many I battle in some ways every day, every hour. Memorizing whole books of the Bible hasn't blanked them out. Reading Scripture each night before bed and spending an hour in prayer daily hasn't drowned them in a typhoon of spirituality. What gives? Am I ignorant?

Am I uncommitted? Am I "unspiritual"? Have I missed it? Do I need to be discipled all over again?

I'm not trying to be pessimistic. Certainly, I won't stop fighting. But it comes down to a basic insight about our condition as Christian people. We're in a war. Staying in the battle, keeping the faith, fighting the fight, and running our course is all far more important to our Lord than whether we've fallen a thousand or a million times. Yes, sin is serious. Yes, it has consequences. But ultimately, God seems to value faith and commitment far more than whether we've lived "victorious" lives.

BATTLEGROUNDS

Do you perceive the Christian life as a war? It doesn't always seem that way, partly because we can't see machine-gun fire and bombs exploding nearby. But if day by day we strive to grow in holiness and faith, if we share the news of Jesus, if we work to bring righteousness and truth into the places where we work and play, we'll soon find out it's war.

The Bible speaks of this war on several fronts. The first and most obvious pits the spiritual forces of darkness against each of us. Authors like Frank Peretti and Dave Hunt have dramatized this struggle in their fiction. Paul illuminated the principle of war in Ephesians 6:12: "Our struggle is not against flesh and blood, but against the rulers, against the authorities, against the powers of this dark world and against the spiritual forces of evil in the heavenly realms." Paul uses the Greek word *palay* for "struggle." It means "wrestling."

As a former wrestler, I can visualize this contest graphically. You stalk out onto the mat bent on only one goal—pinning your opponent. He can't kill you. But he can overwhelm you, defeat you. It's a personal battle. Your hand slides on his sweat and you smell his breath as you grapple, trying to throw one another. His muscles ripple. You feel the fury leaking from his pores. He wants to destroy you.

Haven't you experienced that inner wrestling in which dark forces seem to fling words, arguments, counterarguments, and enticements through your thoughts? I don't believe demons can read our minds or know our thoughts, but if our spirit engages them in argument, they're able to hear and respond to those thoughts. It's personal, hand-to-hand, mind-to-mind combat. It's a constant inner wrestling.

That lesson was nailed home years ago when I worked as a short-order chef in a motel at a ski resort in Vermont. As a new Christian, I had discovered joy, peace, and love. My heart remained full of song. I felt as though I were Gregory Peck in *The Guns of Navarone,* able to live without fear.

The trouble was this woman I had to work with: Cheryl. She loathed me. Her brown-freckled face burned bright with anger the moment she saw me. I tried to be friendly. Each day at lunch I wrote on the kitchen slate the "soup of the day." Underneath, I penned in a short Scripture verse. A little witness to the pagans. That flipped her switch into full-bore fury. Cheryl would glance at the sign, then propel obscenities and gestures at me that could curdle seawater. She was powerfully built too. I did not doubt that Cheryl's fist on my chin would launch a few teeth through the roof.

Nonetheless, I'd just grin and hang tough.

Still, she roared at me to stop trying to convert her. I plodded on, hoping for a change. One night in fury she wrote obscenities in toothpaste and urine on her mirror. Clearly, she had some severe emotional problems.

One afternoon, I sat reading Hal Lindsey's book, *Satan Is Alive and Well on Planet Earth.* I came to a section about demon possession and as I read, bells began ringing in my mind. Was that it? Was that her problem?

My mind almost in a frenzy, I rushed downstairs to her room and knocked. No answer. I cracked open the door. She lay on her bed, staring at the bunk above her. I said, "Cheryl, I need. . . . "

"Get out of here, you son of a. . . ."

I stepped in. "Cheryl! I think I know how to help you."

"I don't want your %$@!*& help! Now get out."

"No, I won't. You need to trust Jesus Christ or you're going to end up dead."

She sat up and glared at me, but I sputtered the Gospel out as quickly as I could, ready to run out the door the moment she began hurling daggers.

Strangely, the fire in her eyes seemed to die. I moved closer, still talking about how trusting Christ could free us from demons and the power of Satan. Soon I was next to her, my stomach muscles contorting, ready for a blow. Somehow I said, "Cheryl, you have to cry out to Jesus to help you. He's the only way."

Her face twisted, as though some titanic battle were taking place inside her, and then she screamed, "Jesus, please help me!"

I forget all that happened after that, except that I went back to my room, sat down on my bunk still shaking and said, "Lord, I didn't know it before, but this is war, isn't it?"

Cheryl was transformed. She spoke kindly, gently. No more obscenities. She came to a Bible study I led with several others who'd trusted Christ that winter. When the season ended, she thanked me and expressed a desire to keep in touch.

That experience gave me great insight about this war we're in. It's all around us, both inside and outside. Demonic forces lob poisoned darts from every angle. They probe for holes and chinks in our defenses. They seek to fell us for good, or at least hamstring us so that we can make no spiritual progress.

"Our struggle is not against flesh and blood."

No, it's inside us. It's a spiritual battle.

How do you get on the winning team?

I always liked the answer of an African chief who became a Christian and frequently discussed the spiritual life with his missionary friends. One night they spoke about temptation, and the chief told how he solved the problem. "I find that deep down inside me there's a big black dog and a big white dog. They fight all the time about everything. The big black dog wants me to do evil things. And the big white dog fights to get me to choose the good."

"So which one wins?" the missionary asked.

The chief replied, "Whichever one I feed the most."

Inside us, the spiritual powers of the world, the flesh, and the devil all work on behalf of evil. But there's also the Holy Spirit and the new nature pushing for good. In the middle is the Christian. All these forces fight to get the Christian's attention. But which ones win?

The ones he feeds the most. If he gives most of his attention to the world, the flesh, and the devil, feeds them, listens to them, and cultivates them, naturally they will win. But if he concentrates his thoughts, inclinations, and impressions on the world of the Spirit and the new nature, these ways will appear much more compelling. Feeding our minds on prayer, the Word of God, fellowship, church, and good deeds gives us the key to winning over temptation.

FIVE STARTING THOUGHTS ABOUT TEMPTATION

Let me give you several thoughts about temptation.

First, while Christ has broken Satan's power, He has not terminated the devil's activity in the world and in our lives. Certainly, God limits what the devil can do to us and with us. The same hedge God erected around Job protects each of us. The devil can't touch us unless God gives him permission. However, while the devil may not strike us physically, his power to suggest and entice seems unlimited.

Herman Wouk's book, *The Caine Mutiny,* tells the powerful story of a mutiny that occurs aboard a minesweeper during World War II. The chief officer, Merrick, gradually loses confidence in his commander, Captain Queeg, through a series of bizarre events. A typhoon begins and threatens to capsize the ship. Captain Queeg freezes at the worst point, unable to give a command. Merrick, believing Queeg is mentally ill, mutinies and takes command. At that moment, the seaman at the helm becomes confused. On the one hand, Captain Queeg screams at him to keep on a forward heading with the wind. Merrick yells to come about and take a reverse heading into the wind. The seaman finally turns to Ensign Keith, a friend of Merrick's and the third in command at that moment. He asks Keith, "What do I do?" Keith tells him to listen to Merrick, and the mutiny is on.

That is our situation. As the seaman at the helm, we have complete control of the ship, that is, our bodies. But several different beings order us to obey them: the world, the flesh, the devil, the Spirit, and the new nature. It's us—the seamen, the Christians—who must choose whom we'll listen to. And it's the one to whom we're more loyal—the one whom we feed the most—whom we'll be most inclined to follow.

Second, as we grow in Christ and become more ef-

fective, Satan targets us for specific attention. As a young Christian, I found many temptations disappeared easily and immediately. Drugs, drinking, sexual immorality, swearing, and several others simply flew out the door.

Other temptations, though, drifted in to replace them. They became far more difficult to dislodge. I didn't even know I had a temper till I got married and had children. Now it's a problem I must work hard at controlling all the time.

Similarly, sexual lust can seem even more ominous after marriage than before. One man told me, "Before I was married, I was a Christian and had little experience with sex. As a result, my fantasies were limited to that experience. But after getting married and experiencing much that sex has to offer, I find that my mind can whoosh off into all sorts of fantasies over other women. Experience—even good experience—gives you more lustful grist for the sexual mill."

As we grow, God opens our eyes up to sins we're committing that we didn't even know were sins. For years I had no idea how much I try to manipulate and threaten people. Then the Spirit of God pointed it out to me. I caught myself with my six-year-old daughter one day. She was angry that I made her clean up her room. Stomping off in a huff, she cried, "Then I won't be your friend anymore!" I laughed, but five minutes later, I heard myself saying to her, "If you don't finish this job, there will be no more McDonald's for you—ever again!" She yelled back in typical womanly fashion, "Yeah, well, I didn't want to go with you anyway." It was then I realized what was happening, and I took her in my arms and said, "Look, honey, I'd like you to clean up your room. So what can we do to get you to do it?"

She murmured with head bowed, "Be nice to me."

I nodded and she went to it. Ten minutes later, we all clapped at the wonder she'd performed in transforming that toy-strewn dump into an organized dream.

Third, Satan and his cohorts are sly, sharp, cunning, and shrewd, but they don't know precisely what your weaknesses are. I tend to think of the devil as virtually omniscient. He knows my every move, thought, and whimper.

But in actuality, the only reason he knows anything about

us is because he studies us constantly. I believe each of us has personal demons assigned to tempt and deceive us as best they can. Obviously, some demons are better than others. Undoubtedly, some effective Christians must face whole "tempt teams" bent on their destruction. But demons, like any other military force, must gather intelligence to find out where the weak points are. They don't automatically know what will fell or even attract us. Thus, they often shoot anything they can at us until they discover what shots ring the bell.

We're not dealing with an enemy who has all knowledge, all power, and all influence at his fingertips. He's only as powerful as we're willing to let him become.

Fourth, Satan works over the long haul. He's in it for life—your life and mine. As a result, he must work inch by inch, block by block. With truly effective Christians living in the power of the Spirit, he may take years to wear down their resistance to sin. He has no idea how he can muster the particular forces to knock us down. But he labors and prepares so that when the right opportunity occurs, he's ready.

Take the experience of David and Bathsheba. I honestly don't think the devil engineered the circumstances that led to David's fall. But the powers of darkness did influence David to become lazy, bored, and overwhelmed by lust. He had many wives by that time, in direct disobedience to Scripture. Demonic forces struggled to wean him away from composing psalms and being intimate with God. They knew it was only a matter of time before the right circumstances came together. When Bathsheba bathed naked and beautiful in sight of the king, the demons needed only whisper a few suggestive phrases before David was thinking adulterous thoughts.

The devil moves us in sinful directions by degrees. A swear word there. A compromise about traffic laws here. A prolonged gaze at a comely female over there. Over the course of a few years, or even months, he can guide an unwitting Christian into sinful behavior. The old story of the mammoth sequoia felled not by lightning, fire, or earthquake, but by the termites burrowing through its trunk is no myth. If Satan could unleash sin with a blitzkrieg attack, he probably would. But in most circumstances, he must resort to using the tunnel under the fortress and the termite in the wood. **Fifth, there's no mysterious secret to winning over temptation.** God has not penned some flashy, memorable formula for success. We can't wave a wand over sin and make it disappear. We must make a lifetime of imbibing the Word of God and rigorously applying it in the day-by-day wrestlings of existence. Secrets are for dreamers. If anything, God wants us to be flint-eyed warriors willing to march miles through muck to reach our destination.

For years I have battled the problem of eating more than I need. I love devouring Ben and Jerry's Cherry Garcia ice cream at 200 calories or so a spoonful. I can clean up a batch of Godiva chocolates in a matter of lickety-split. But the secret of losing weight isn't the wisdom of Dr. Pritikin, Dr. Stillman, or the latest Hollywood starlet diet; it's eating less, exercising more. In other words, pain! There's no marvelous method to make it easy. I must make a sheer, tooth-rattling refusal to gorge myself.

Similarly, a person I know frequently fights the impulse to watch a video when he should be preparing messages. Thoughts of enjoying the great scenes from *Gone with the Wind* and *Star Wars* flash through his mind. But again, he knows there's no secret. A simple, "No, I won't," and a decision to continue working is the answer. No pill, psychological mind play, or catchy phrase will make it any easier.

I like what the little boy said when he came home from swimming in the creek. His mother had warned him in sure and certain terms that he would be severely punished if he went in again. He clattered in the door with his hair damp and his body soaked, but his clothes were dry. "You went in the creek," his mother said.

"I fell in accidentally," said the boy.

"Then why aren't your clothes wet?"

"I took them off because I was afraid I might fall in."

Isn't that the way it is? We lure ourselves into temptation instead of simply running away.

We're in a war. The devil's effort to prevent our sanctification is all out. He will take no prisoners and offer no quarter. He wants nothing less than your soul, your whole soul, and nothing but your soul.

Does it sound bad?

Absolutely. But remember, soldiers don't tell fairy tales around the campfire at night after the battle; they tell war stories. When I get to heaven, I hope you'll have a few to tell me, because I know I've got several I'd like to share with you.

WHAT ON EARTH IS SATAN TRYING TO DO?

CHAPTER 2

Butch Cassidy's gang stops the train and packs dynamite on the hinges of the door of the Western Union car. When the safe explodes, dollar bills fly everywhere. Cowboys scurry around, retrieving the precious bills. But suddenly on the horizon another train appears. A black engine chugs into view with two sinister, coal-black armored cars behind it. It stops, black smoke belching from its stack. Then the doors open and a posse of bullet-eyed, single-minded men on huge steeds bolt down the ramps, bent on capture.

Butch stares at Sundance, and they both leap onto their horses, forgetting the money. They gallop for the hills with the lawmen on their heels. The posse consists of an Indian with a nose for tracking, a cocksure marshall in a white straw hat, and several others. They don't look friendly.

Butch and Sundance split off from their gang, thinking the posse also will separate. But the horsemen don't even swerve in the gang's direction. "What's wrong with them?" Butch cries, desperate to get away from what he knows will be a relentless, unto-death pursuit.

They cover their tracks, trot over an untraveled plateau, and even jump horses, letting one riderless horse canter off in another direction—all to no avail. Nothing works. Every few tricks Butch stops, turns around, and gasps, "Who are those guys?"

The movie *Butch Cassidy and the Sundance Kid* depicts the hunted and the hunter in all its comic and tragic detail. In the end, all the tricks fail. Butch and Sundance's hunters finally corner them in a canyon, and only by leaping a hundred feet into the river below do they escape.

I see in this movie an analogy to the Christian life. The devil, like that posse, pursues us relentlessly. He probes, pushes, pummels, and plunders us with fuming malice. Nothing less than capitulation will satisfy him. For him, temptation is the weapon of choice for the war unto death.

How do you beat your enemy? By knowing him, his habits, his ploys, his ways and means, and motivations.

Prior to World War II, Winston Churchill's warnings did little more than make the politicians laugh. As early as 1924 he began watching the rise of Adolph Hitler. He studied newspapers and dispatches out of Germany. During the 1930s, he warned the world that Hitler thirsted only to avenge the Allies' shameful Treaty of Versailles, an agreement where Germany was forced to accept impossible and even despicable terms of surrender at the end of World War I. He alone seemed to understand what motivated Hitler. That knowledge enabled him later to hold Britain steady during Germany's assault in World War II, and to lead the British Commonwealth to victory.

Knowing what motivates an enemy, understanding what he wishes to accomplish can help us to resist his onslaught with greater will. If we know a bully wants only the mint in our shirt pocket, we might give it to him without a fight. But when we realize he prefers to cut our throat, then we may choose to defend ourselves at any cost.

Satan invented temptation for a purpose. To him it's no game. He used temptation first in heaven to rile angels into rebellion. Then he employed the same tactic in the Garden to deceive Eve. By questioning the woman's understanding of

God's command, Satan opened a Pandora's box of unspeak-able pain—from Cain's murder of Abel to Amnon's rape of his sister Tamar and the crucifixion of the Son of God, to those of more recent times—Pol Pot's genocide in Cambodia and Nicolae Ceausescu's mass murder of Rumania's life and spirit, we see the results of Satan's deeds.

Every sin that ever occurred started with a small, simple, and subtle temptation that looked at best harmless, and at worst, forgivable. But temptation always leads somewhere. Like any story, it has a beginning, middle, and end.

What is Satan trying to accomplish?

We can look at his purpose on two levels. First, the human. In the next chapter, we'll look at his efforts to hinder God.

HOW TEMPTATION AFFECTS HUMANS
By leading us into sin, the devil destroys our confi-dence in God's ability to help us. The devil is never content merely to knock us down. No, he wants to grind our nose into the mat, mash us through the floor, make us eat the dirt underneath, and then kick us all the way down the street. Before we give in to temptation, the devil coos, "One fall won't hurt; you can always get up again." After we fall though, he towers over us with a whip, shrieking, "You can never get up again; you're given over to it. Give up!"

Guilt decimates a Christian's effectiveness. Satan knows that guilt keeps a person from God, even when she under-stands His provision for sin. Adam and Eve made leaf aprons and cowered in the trees. King David's limbs seared with fever after his sin with Bathsheba, and he pled with God for release. Judas Iscariot committed suicide. Peter, even after Jesus appeared to him following his three denials, convinced himself he was unworthy; he returned to his past life of fishing.

David spoke profoundly of the condition. "For day and night Your hand was heavy upon me; my strength was sapped as in heat of summer" (Ps. 32:4). We perceive God as the enemy, rather than the healing doctor ready to bind up our wounds at our feeblest call.

The worst result of falling into sin is not the need for forgiveness; it's the belief that you're stuck, sunk, buried by your sin; you believe you will never escape; even God can't help you.

While I was in seminary, a friend of mine wrestled with a terrible problem that caused him anger and bitterness. At one point he sat alone in his bedroom and pointed a cocked pistol at his temple. The despair in his soul that even God could not help him pushed him to the edge of disaster. Fortunately, he could not pull the trigger and later sought help.

Many Christians fight the belief that God has rejected them. The devil works overtime to push us into that dark vault. Through temptation, the devil mires us in sin until we believe even God cannot help us.

Satan seeks to destroy our ability to witness and serve. Nothing kills witness faster than sin. Satan tempted Timothy to believe he couldn't do the job because he was too young and inexperienced. He stopped seeking out converts, preaching the Word, and fulfilling his ministry. Paul had to encourage him not to be ashamed (see 2 Tim. 1:8-9).

Non-Christians excuse their unbelief because of the sin they observe in Christians. It's not an excuse that God accepts, but it's also one we should avoid giving unbelievers. It's like a story I read in the paper some years ago. Irene Phillips of Haddenham, England ripped open a package of frozen peas and out clunked a frog. After getting her money back from the local supermarket, she commented, "It was the most revolting thing I have ever seen. Even one of its legs was missing!" A spokesman for the supermarket promised to investigate, but he responded, "It wasn't such a *big* frog."

Incredible as that story is, isn't that precisely what we Christians often do? When some unbeliever remarks about some pet sin of ours—our frog in the frozen peas—we say, "It isn't such a big sin." Meanwhile, Satan revels in it. It's a double whammy because such weakness keeps us from sharing our faith and gives unbelievers an excuse not to believe.

The devil knows that a first sin moves us in the direction of a second and third sin. Cain's first sin wasn't murdering Abel; rather, both his attitude and offering displeased God: "But on Cain and his offering He did not look with favor" (Gen. 4:5). The devil tempted him to believe God required too much. He brought shoddy crops when the time came to give the gift. Some say Cain's sin lay in not bringing a blood offering. But nothing in the text indicates Cain was required to offer such a gift. I believe what God seemed to spurn was a rotten, second-rate gift. Cain didn't bring his best crops, but the withered, useless ones. He wanted to be done with that offering business and get on with life.

Nonetheless, when God rejected Cain's gift, his anger ignited, and he went to Abel for support. Abel agreed with God. "You're wrong, Cain. Just do what God says, and all will be well." That was the stick of dynamite that exploded inside Cain, and he murdered Abel. The devil must have fueled his attitude for years. The sin of murder was preceded by a long list of sins of pride, hatred, malice, envy, and jealousy.

Satan knows sin will harden our hearts. Hebrews 12:15 says, "See to it that no one misses the grace of God and that no bitter root grows up to cause trouble and defile many." The author gives the illustration of Esau, who so scorned his birthright and the truth of God that he hardened his heart beyond hope. The text says he "found no room for repentance." In other words, he knew it was wrong, but he could not drum up the conviction or resolution to repent.

Hardness of heart does that. One person told me that when he becomes entrenched in a sin, he also becomes unwilling to listen compassionately to his wife and undisciplined in his daily routine. Lust permeates his thoughts. A hardness creeps over his thoughts and emotions. He begins defending his sin. Finally, he becomes judgmental toward others about the same sin!

But a severe reaction also results. He loses all sense of joy and peace.

God has placed a "hardness-of-heart meter" inside all of us. When we find ourselves void of joy, peace, and genuine love for others, we can be sure we have developed a callous spirit.

Filippo Brunelleschi (1377–1446), one of Italy's greatest architects and engineers, crowned his life's work by designing the famed dome of the Florence cathedral. To build that dome, he constructed numerous machines never known before. But he had a problem. The cathedral stood on marshy ground. The foundation was weak. To check for problems he provided a small opening in the ceiling. A shaft of sunlight through that hole would cover a brass plate on the floor of the sanctuary only on July 21. If the patch of light failed to cover the plate perfectly, it indicated the dome had tilted.

In the same way, the Spirit fills the Christian's heart with every good fruit: "Love, joy, peace, patience, kindness, goodness, faithfulness, gentleness, and self-control" (Gal. 5:22-23). When we find these attitudes and actions disappearing from our lives, hardness has set in. This is precisely what Satan desires, for hardness of heart leads to a poor testimony, slackness in service, and misery of heart that puts the saint out of commission.

Sin will keep us from growing and learning to discern. Hebrews 5:13-14 reminds us that practicing righteousness trains us "to discern good and evil." It is not just knowing the Word of God that helps us grow; practicing it nurtures the attitudes, habits, and lifestyle that enable us to perceive God's will in the murky situations of life. Sin lashes blinders to our eyes. It confuses and upsets us. Ultimately, it paves the path to more foolish and sinful decisions. We cease to grow and develop as God-honoring Christians.

Have you ever visited a lake and noticed submerged pieces of wood on the bottom? Wood floats, doesn't it? So how did it end up on the bottom? It became waterlogged. Immersion in the lake over a long period of time soaked the wood so thoroughly that it finally sank.

The devil's strategy calls for leading us into sin, turning that sin into a habit, and finally sinking us through guilt and remorse. He turns us into submarine Christians: running silent and deep, not touching anyone on the surface of life.

Sin will keep us from gaining God's true riches. After Moses grew up in Pharaoh's palace, he decided to cast his lot with his Hebrew brethren. At the time he possessed every advantage and benefit. But he rejected it all in order to identify himself with the people of God. Hebrews 11:24-26 confirms the principle: "By faith Moses, when he had grown up, refused to be known as the son of Pharaoh's daughter. He chose to be mistreated along with the people of God rather than to enjoy the pleasures of sin for a short time. He regarded disgrace for the sake of Christ as of greater value than the treasures of Egypt, because he was looking ahead to his reward."

Notice what Moses rejected: "the pleasures of sin for a short time." In other words, the Bible recognizes sin is pleasurable; that pleasure passes quickly however.

Look also at what Moses sought: "his reward." Real riches come through obeying and loving God, not through abandoning yourself to sin. Satan's lie continues today: "Follow me, and I will give you pleasures galore. Follow God, and you'll gain nothing but pain." Once the first rush passes, sin bestows none of the true riches of life, but only guilt, dissolution, destruction, and death.

Sin will lead us into a condition of spiritual and possibly physical death. In 1 Corinthians 11:30, Paul notes that many of the Christians at Corinth were "weak and sick" and a number were dead. Why? Because of sin. Satan's realm is the realm of death. Only there can he experience a semblance of pleasure. Leading us into sin unleashes the degraded joy he longs for. Our spiritual death and despondency is his sodden victory over God.

Death is a condition of separation. For the Christian, sin imposes a kind of death: a cleavage in our fellowship with God. We cease to experience His friendship and presence. He seems distant, uncaring, even an enemy who convicts and harangues us for our offenses. Through temptation, Satan separates good friends—the Christian and God. He turns them into arguing, complaining mates who inhabit the same house but can't enjoy its delights.

Sin keeps us from choosing the things that are excellent. Paul informed the Philippians that he prayed their "love might abound more and more in knowledge and depth of insight, so that you may be able to discern what is best and may be pure and blameless until the day of Christ" (Phil. 1:9-10).

Dr. Howard Hendricks, professor emeritus at Dallas Theological Seminary, used to tell his classes, "The problem in knowing God's will for the Christian is not knowing the difference between what is right and what is wrong. That's often rather simple. Rather it's discerning the difference between what is good and what is better, and between what is better and what is best." Deliberating between black and white poses little difficulty. It's the white, the off-white, and the cream that stymie us. What is best for us, and how do we find it?

Sin will cloud the issue. It drags a fog into our minds and shrouds our spiritual eyes in mist. We grope about, unable to choose the best in life. We opt for those things which might be good, but which fail to yield the true riches.

Committing sin can cause us to lead others astray. Paul concluded his words on the spiritual descent of man in Romans 1 with the saddest truth of all. As we slip into the slime, we love nothing more than pulling a few others down with us. Romans 1:32 says, "Although they know God's righteous decree that those who do such things deserve death, they not only continue to do these very things but also approve of those who practice them."

Even Christians fall into such behavior. One man I know refuses to obey speed limits and even uses a radar-detection device he calls a "fuzz-buster." On a few occasions I've listened to his hearty speeches on how effective and helpful his copper-stopper is. I thought at one point to mention that such behavior might rank as sin. But instead, I actually considered buying one myself. Because he did it, I felt it might be all right.

Similarly, a man I interviewed refused to drink alcohol for years. But then he noticed a number of Christian friends who enjoyed their beer and cocktails, and for that reason he decided to try it. In a matter of months, he became enmeshed in a habit of drinking whenever it was offered. Convicted about it, he stopped. He realized how susceptible he was to the example of other Christians. When we see people practicing something we might consider off-limits, it's much easier to give in, even against reason, biblical statements, and long-established tradition and opinion.

Finally, giving in to sin leads us to tolerate other sin in our midst. The Corinthians involved themselves in a number of sins, including forming cliques and factions, taking one another to court, getting drunk at the Lord's Supper, using temple prostitutes, and rejecting the truth of the Resurrection. But Paul denounced them most for their toleration of incest between a member and his father's second wife. In fact, they proudly advertised their views on this issue. In effect, their own guilt and sinfulness led them to condone all other forms of sin.

As I write, I know of a Bible-believing church where a member of the board of elders, a woman, is conducting an affair with a former pastor. Another church includes a member who is known as "the most corrupt lawyer in town." A third has allowed several couples who claim to be Christians to divorce so they can marry other members of the same church.

Why do such things go on? Because Christians won't confront the sin outright. Why? Often it's because speaking out against sin might arouse others to point out our own ugly blemishes.

One of Aesop's fables features a fox who, upon seeing a lion for the first time, was so terrified he nearly died. The second time he met the lion he quaked, but he managed to disguise it and passed by quickly without a cry. However, the third time he saw the lion, he felt so bold that he bounded up to the beast and asked him, "How do you do?" Aesop's moral is, of course, "Familiarity breeds contempt."

In the spiritual realm, toleration of sin breeds multiplication of sin. Paul told the Corinthians that "bad company corrupts good character" (1 Cor. 15:33) and "a little yeast works through the whole batch of dough" (5:6). Satan knows that getting one to sin will affect others. In this way, he can injure a whole congregation's witness and fellowship.

THE DEVIL'S PLAN

Leading a Christian into sin enables the devil to achieve many low and dirty goals. Ultimately, he believes he can foil and foul God's plan beyond redemption.

Fortunately, Scripture reveals he can't do this. God's purpose will never be overturned by Satan, no matter how hard he huffs and puffs. God can still work for good in the midst of the most destructive sins (Rom. 8:28). But that does not mean God will lift the consequences of our crimes.

Years ago, Dr. Haddon Robinson, now a professor at Gordon-Conwell Seminary in Massachusetts, spoke of a friend of his who served and ministered in a large, effective church. The pastor was tempted and led into adultery. It destroyed his marriage, family life, and ministry. Dr. Robinson asked the man at one point, "What can I carry back to the young men at seminary? What should I tell them about your experience?"

Through tearful eyes, the former pastor said, "Tell them this: when you cease to walk with God, you walk on the edge of an abyss."

Every one of Satan's grand plans is squashed by one basic truth of Scripture: When we walk with God, we can never stumble so as to destroy our lives. David wrote in Psalm 37:23-24: "The Lord delights in the way of the man whose steps He has made firm; though he stumble, he will not fall, for the Lord upholds him with His hand."

The words of Jude are another potent assurance: "Now to Him who is able to keep you from stumbling, and to make you stand in the presence of His glory blameless with great joy" (Jude 24).

As we walk with the Lord, our sin becomes less useful to the devil's plans. When we fall—and we will—we aren't hurled headlong into space to be dashed upon sharp, unyielding rocks. Rather, our Lord holds us, firm and stable. We trust that He will lead us through.

So long as we have that outlook and that attitude, the devil can claim no power over us. He can whisper his taunts and sling his fiery balls of temptation, but nothing can permanently fell us.

Yet, cease to walk with God, and we walk on the edge of an abyss.

SATAN'S STRATEGY AGAINST GOD

CHAPTER 3

Satan flung at God's feet the grandest challenge in history when he roared those weighty words found in Isaiah 14:13-14:

I will ascend to heaven;
I will raise my throne above the stars of God;
I will sit on the mount of assembly, of the utmost heights of the sacred mountain.
I will ascend above the tops of the clouds;
I will make myself like the Most High.

This fivefold threat reveals much about the pride, arrogance, self-confidence, and self-deception of Satan. In the context, he appears to speak these words after being deposed from his position as God's mightiest angel. He stands as an outcast, having no authority or voice in the administration of heaven, though he still has access to it.

What Satan swore was nothing less than the annihilation of

God. He would retake his throne in heaven, destroy all opposition from God's loyal angels and enslave them, stand in God's stead at the assembly place of the universe, and dispatch Him once and for all. It was a vicious and vengeful boast, even though God could have laughed in his face the same way the sun might laugh at a speck that threatened to extinguish its light.

God prevented Satan from inflicting further damage in heaven. He secured the hearts of the remaining angels. Then He decided to fabricate a whole new universe and place at its center a being created in His image. Satan turned his eyes on that new creature and decided, "If I can't beat Him on His own turf, I'll destroy His creations and make them my slaves. I'll bring Him to His knees through His precious children."

We saw in the previous chapter what Satan seeks to accomplish through temptation in the lives of God's people. But what are his strategies against God? What does he want to achieve on a supernatural level?

FIGHTING GOD

The most obvious purpose of Satan's offensive is to fight and frustrate God. Satan believes that by hurting God's people he hurts God. In a war, such tactics are common. The Nazis, for instance, would attack a town and, in order to get the Resistance to talk, they would capture and torture the daughter of its commanding officer. The logic is as old as Satan himself. You coerce the father by harming the son. You bring the mother to her knees by holding the lighted cigarette to the rosy cheek of the six-year-old daughter.

Is God moved or frightened by these tactics? Not really. Satan can't touch a single saint unless God allows it. He has provided a complete and final redemption in Christ that eliminates Satan's only real threat, which is death. God has placed a hedge around every one of His children that prevents the devil from laying a talon on them.

Thus, Satan's fight becomes a source of incredible frustration to him. This is why I believe Peter says that the devil "prowls about like a roaring lion, looking for someone to devour" (1 Peter 5:8). Imagine a lion in a zoo lusting for blood. He spots a whole crowd of saints standing outside the bars. He roars, paws, threatens, taunts, then crashes into the fence in fury, knocking himself silly. When the dizziness passes, he gets up and roars again in rage. But he can't get through. An iron hedge protects the people from him.

In the same way, the spiritual world must look to the devil like a maze of hideous hedges keeping him away from the saints. While he can still tempt them, he can't touch them. He lurches about in a frenzy, determined to break through somewhere, but possessing no power to do it.

I suspect that Satan and his cohorts are highly frustrated beings. While they can lure us into sin, simple confession and repentance breaks the hold. He may be able to huff his fetid breath into our faces, but he can't blow our houses down. He can't hurt God personally or through His people.

And yet, he fights on. He can read the Bible and see his end, but he doesn't believe it. He chooses to believe his own lie — that somehow he can defeat God.

The problem for us is that it can appear that Satan has won ground against God. Look at the world. We shudder to see the murder, strife, divorce, hatred, rape, greed, theft, and genocide that run wild around us. But while the whole world "lies in the power of the evil one," as 1 John 5:19 says, it's also true that "greater is He who is in you than he who is in the world" (1 John 4:4). Satan fights on futilely. He won't stop. But he's like the boxer who though knocked out, stands up and spits from his corner, declaring he's been cheated. The fight's over, but the yelling and intimidation aren't.

HE TRIES TO PROVE TO GOD WE DON'T LOVE HIM
A second purpose Satan has in tempting us is to show the results to God as proof that we don't love Him. When Satan tromped into the heavenly assembly pictured in Job 1, God asked him if he'd seen Job during his travels. God was especially interested in whether he noticed Job's devotion, that he was "blameless and upright, a man who fears God and shuns evil" (Job 1:8). Satan's answer illuminates classically his attitude about all people committed to Christ: they love God only because of what He gives them. "Stretch out Your hand and strike everything he has, and he will surely curse You to Your face" (1:11).

In other words, no one loves God because He is good, holy, and worthy of such love; we love Him only for what we get out of Him. Stop the flow of the goodies, and God's people will head for another religion.

Each time Satan tempts us, he challenges God: "If this saint goes my way, it proves he doesn't really love You." Every fall to temptation is in effect a slap in the face of God. We declare, "I choose Satan's way rather than Yours."

But confession of sin and repentance turn the whole argument around. When a Christian sins, the Spirit will discipline him. He repents, confesses his guilt, and renews his fellowship with the Lord. Perhaps for this reason, Satan hates repentance and contrition even more than a Christian's living in perfect righteousness. For through our repentance, God displays His forgiveness, grace, love, and mercy, all of which sting the nostrils of the devil.

Furthermore, while Satan believes falling to temptation proves we don't love God, it's another form of self-deception. God knows where, when, and how we will fall even before we do; as a result, He plans to work around it and even turn it for good in our lives.

SATAN TRIES TO RUIN GOD'S PLAN

A third purpose Satan has in temptation is the complete ruin of God's eternal plan. Satan believes that by leading us into sin he will wreck God's plan and send Him scurrying back to His blueprint room, desperate to find a way to stave off complete disaster. This is one more form of self-deception which Satan could easily rectify by reading a few verses from the Bible. "He spoke, and it came to be; He commanded, and it stood firm. . . . The plans of the Lord stand firm forever, the purposes of His heart through all generations" (Ps. 33:9, 11). God cannot be overtaken, overturned, or overwhelmed. But Satan believes he is capable of doing it anyway.

How can this be? Doesn't Satan know the Bible? Doesn't he realize all his efforts will come to nothing?

Of course he knows the Bible. Presumably he has at least some familiarity with it, even though I honestly do not think he pays much attention to it. Satan is a liar. And the worst thing about lying is not that you come to believe everything you lie about, but that in the end you can't believe anyone else. I believe Satan refuses to accept that what God says *is* true. Certainly he understands that God claims absolute sovereignty over every person, event, thought, word, and deed. Certainly he sees that he cannot even tempt a saint apart from God's permission. But that doesn't matter. Satan lies to his followers and lies to himself. He has convinced himself that leading us into temptation foils God's plan, even though God's plan already compensates for every plot Satan dreams up.

It's necessary to understand the mind of Satan as we face this problem of temptation. His mind is twisted and deceived by his own lies. Satan reads the truth only so he can contradict it and twist it to suit his own purposes.

Someone once asked me, "If Satan knows what it says in the Book of Revelation about being chained and confined to hell forever and ever, why doesn't he give up? Why does he fight on?"

Very simply, I suspect he refuses to believe that's the way it will be. Remember, he sees history unfold the same way we do, one second at a time. He doesn't know the future except as it's revealed in the Bible.

I remember reading about a farmer who had never seen a movie. His son bought a projector and showed him a film of a train wreck. As the film unreeled, the farmer watched in amazement as the trains steamed down the tracks. A lone engineer tried to flip the switch that would keep them from colliding. But his efforts failed. The trains crashed.

After the movie, the son retired to his bedroom. Later he heard his father yelling in the parlor. He went downstairs only to find the man replaying the movie over and over, trying to get the engineer to succeed and keep the trains from wrecking.

"Dad, what are you doing?" the son called.

"Trying to stop the train wreck!" he said, as he shouted one more time at the engineer.

"You can't stop it, Dad. It's a movie. It's on the film."

The old man looked around sheepishly, then said, "Well, what good is it then if you can't do nothin' about it?"

The devil's like that old farmer, except that he still believes he can get the engineer's trains onto parallel tracks. But all of history is like an already-finished movie to God. His plan can't be altered. It will press on to its conclusion without a glitch. Only fools will try to fight it. And Satan, unfortunately, is the greatest fool of all.

SATAN TRIES TO PROVE HIS WAY IS BETTER

A fourth purpose Satan has in tempting us is to prove his way is better. Why did God allow Satan to continue his rebellion after that first sin in heaven? He could have destroyed the devil then and there. He might have confined him forever in hell, never to peep again. But God chose to allow evil to run its course. In effect, He said, "All right, Satan, you think your way is better. Then you do what you wish and I will work My plan in the midst of it. In the end, we'll see who has the better way."

Why did God do this? I believe because Satan won a third of heaven in the first rebellion (see Rev. 12:4). If God had destroyed all those rebels, how would this prevent another rebellion from happening, and then another, and another? If God didn't give Satan the chance to show the foolishness of life apart from His presence, He would have continuous rebellions on His hands.

Through temptation, the devil seeks to prove that his way is the better way. We see this all over the media. Most of what unfurls before us in the world reflects the extent of Satan's dominion. He's trying every way he can to prove that his wisdom exceeds God's. He does it by tempting us to go his way.

But what do we actually see in the world? If anything, nothing less than complete confusion! That's precisely the problem. Satan is thoroughly confused. He doesn't know what will work and what won't. So he tries everything! Anything, so long as it's not God's way, is acceptable.

I see this happening in publishing. As an aspiring author of fiction, I try to keep up to date on what Christians are writing. In publishing talk, there's a kind of book called a "crossover" book. It's a title that crosses over from the mainstream market to the religious, or vice-versa. An older example of this were some of Catherine Marshall's books — *Christy* and *A Man Called Peter*. Both were religious, and yet reached a mainstream audience. More recent examples are the biography of pitching star Orel Hershiser entitled *Out of the Blue* and many of Robert Schuller's books.

Some editors have encouraged me to try to write "crossover" fiction, the kind that will find a niche in the mainstream while still appealing to Christians. I've read a lot of such books, and one recently that struck me was a teenage romance about two friends, one of whom is dying of cancer. The book moved me to tears. The author wrote the story masterfully. It also had a lot of upbeat thoughts about God. What it didn't have was any mention of Christ, life through faith in Him, or recognition of sin.

Now I'm not saying every novel should be a proclamation of the Gospel. But to give teens hope of life beyond the grave based on some vague notion of God is a snare of the devil. A teen could read that book and think, "Oh, so all I need do is believe He's there and that He loves me and I'm all right." One can be a Buddhist or a Hindu and believe those things.

The media is presently assaulting us with movies about death and life beyond death. Movies like *Always, Ghost, Flatliners, Indiana Jones and the Last Crusade, E.T.,* and even *Return of the Jedi* portray a worldview of eternal life that encourages people to think all are acceptable, there's nothing to be afraid of, just believe, and you'll be okay. But believe what? A worldview that leaves out Christ, leaves out redemption, leaves out repentance, sanctification, holiness, worship, and everything else. In other words, Satan's worldview.

Satan is seeking to show that his way is better. He doesn't care what way we take so long as it's not the Way, the Truth, and the Life. Satan is, I believe, setting up millions of people for the grand illusion — the belief that mankind can make it on its own without God.

USING EVIDENCE AGAINST US

A fifth purpose Satan has toward defeating God is to gain evidence against us so he can accuse us before God. Satan is the great accuser of God's people (Rev. 12:10). Leading us into sin gives Satan evidence of our lack of faith, our appalling weaknesses, and our insidious hidden sins that we think no one knows about. Just as Satan accused Job of having no genuine love for God, so he accuses us of the same sin to God's face. I'm sure one of his cohorts is up there right now reeling off long lists of my own crimes against God Himself. He wants to show once and for all that both you and I are complete failures, worthy only of hell.

Fortunately, God simply turns to Jesus at His right hand and asks, "Is he one of Yours?" Jesus nods and the devil slumps. But he still rushes back tomorrow with new and improved charges of the same old sins, hoping somehow he'll land on one God can't forgive. He's the quintessential tattletale.

My father used to have a favorite expression when one of his three children would bound in with some tidbit about a sibling's misbehavior. Before we finished the first sentence, he'd say, "Who do you worry about?"

We'd roll our eyes and say, "Me."

"OK, then I don't need to hear this, correct?"

"Correct."

Like those tattling little kids, Satan comes back time and again to the throne of God with the truth — for once — about us. Indeed, we are a wretched, corruptible, cantankerous, and contemptible bunch. We sin sixteen hours a day in thought, word, and deed (and if we sin while dreaming, twenty-four), and the devil writes it all down. Then he proceeds to the throne room of God, thinking he's found the transgression that will condemn us for good. And the Father just sighs and looks at Jesus, and the charges are dismissed. Satan retreats in defeat once more.

Why does he do it?

More self-deception. He simply doesn't understand the nature of forgiveness and grace. Redemption in Christ is beyond his brain power. He can't comprehend it because he can't experience it.

FIRE INSURANCE
Finally, I believe Satan through temptation and sin is trying to purchase fire insurance against final judgment. First Corinthians 6:3 tells us that we shall judge

angels. One day every angel will appear before the saints, we'll hear all their deeds, and make a pronouncement of punishment. That's incredible, but that's what Paul says we'll do.

What tactic do we use to try to wriggle out of being punished for an infraction? You know it: "What about him? Why, he did worse than me!" We try to find people (or angels) who have sinned worse than us and use them to make ourselves look better. Remember how teachers used to grade on a curve? If the whole class missed all the same questions and no one scored above a 60 out of 100, then the curve makes 60 an A, 50 a B, and so on down the line. Similarly, I suspect Satan believes that if he can get millions of people to reject Christ and live unholy, abject lives, then God will be forced to grade on a curve and let them all out of the punishment. He tells himself, "Surely, God won't punish billions!"

But Satan's fire insurance theory won't ride. God will judge with perfect justice. Those who reject Christ will die in their sins, whether their sins are great or small, many or few.

It's a sorry picture. Satan and his cohorts expend vast amounts of energy trying to maim God and demolish His plan. But He has it all under control. They cannot succeed, and we as Christians cannot fail.

Still, the devil fights on. We're in a war. He will not give up. He continues to try to convince us he can do all of the above and more. What we must keep before us is that Christ our Savior has won an overwhelming victory through the cross. The prince of this world has lost; he just refuses to believe it. Every time we call on the Christ of the cross, though, we remind Satan of his defeat.

OUR PRIMARY ENEMY: THE WORLD, THE FLESH, OR THE DEVIL?

CHAPTER 4

Christians know that the unholy trinity in the lives of all of us is "the world, the flesh, and the devil." These three realities provide the grist for the temptation mill that grinds our lives to mash. How do the three relate?

I believe, as I wrote earlier, that the world provides a deceptive picture. It paints sin in its most alluring and captivating colors. It plays up the pleasures and cancels the consequences. It gives us a come-on, and we respond.

The devil points to those alluring pictures and croons into our consciousness the happiness we'll gain by partaking of them. While the world gives us the product, Satan provides the advertising.

The flesh is that "person" inside us who dances to the world's tune and Satan's lyric. We can call him the old nature. He's a "responder." He sees the picture, hears the ad line, and tells himself, "Yes, I want that."

God has placed in the being of man several things that mitigate the power of temptation. Though the unbeliever sees what the world portrays and even senses the voice of the devil in his mind, the conscience and the law (as well as moral traditions, family, friends, and so on) can keep him from committing any and every sin. This is why unbelievers can be "moral people" to some degree without knowing Christ.

But what does the picture look like for the believer?

The same process is apparent, except the believer has a number of mitigating forces working on his behalf. The flesh is now dead, having died with Christ on the cross (see Rom. 6). The conscience is still active, but it's a new, living conscience, not seared, as can happen with the unbeliever. Moreover, the Christian is dead to the law, which could only condemn him. He no longer has to live with that daily voice of condemnation. But in addition to all this, he has a "new nature" (2 Cor. 5:17) that God has implanted in him. He is a "new creation." God has taken his personality (soul and spirit) and made it new, yet without changing its uniqueness.

Above all, the believer has the Spirit residing within him as well as the Word of God to dwell on, both of which empower, guide, and strengthen him in his daily walk.

Think about it a moment. Haven't you seen all these forces at work in your heart when you face temptation? It might happen something like this:

The world shows a man a picture of a beautiful woman, scantily clad.

The flesh says, "Hey, get a load of this."

Immediately, the conscience kicks in, "No, you shouldn't look at this woman that way."

Instantly, the devil chirps, "What's the big deal? It's only a look."

But the Word we've memorized floods our mind, and we recall we are not to commit adultery, spiritual or physical.

Again the devil counteracts, "Oh, give me a break. You're not about to commit adultery; you're just enjoying the view."

Then the Spirit pops up. "I'd suggest a way of escape in a verse of Scripture you can meditate on."

Finally, the new nature answers, "I think that's what I'll do—meditate on Psalm 1:1 rather than this woman before me."

Such arguments, I believe, can be played out in our minds hundreds of times a day over every conceivable subject and situation. But it's the person with the new nature who makes the choice that leads to victory.

SATAN'S TECHNIQUES

What then can the devil do in trying to destroy us? Scripture says that he practices the following techniques.

Deception and lying (John 8:44). He is the "father of lies." Since God is truth, Satan's only recourse is to take what truth there is and twist it, take it apart, contradict it, lessen it, lighten it, or do any number of things that somehow make it less or more than it is. Satan can never let a real truth stand on its own, unless he uses it so out of context that in a particular situation it is completely false.

Accusation (Rev. 12:10; Zech. 3:1). The devil loves to clobber us with reams of accusations about what failures, sinners, fakes, hypocrites, and "miserable examples" we are as Christians. Amy Grant said recently in an interview, "Satan is the accuser, but what makes his voice so debilitating is the truth in those knowing accusations. So face them head on: 'You're right! You're absolutely right! I'm selfish, I'm self-centered, I have all the wrong motives. I don't even know if anything I'm doing is right! But so what? This is all I've got to start with. It's not what I want to end up being. But all I've got to start with is self-centered, carnal, mixed motive, idiotic me. I've got to start somewhere, and this is the place I've got to start.' "[1]

Temptation (Matt. 4:1-2; Job 1–2). All of Satan's tactics work together for his main purpose—to tempt us and entice us to commit sins and engage in activities we know God says are wrong.

Thwarting and hindering (1 Thes. 2:18). Though God is sovereign, for reasons known only to Him, He does allow Satan to "hinder" us from carrying out our personal plans and goals.

Sifting (Luke 22:31-34; Job 1–2). Satan constantly demands the opportunity to "sift" us like wheat. That is, he wants to

[1]Dale Hanson Bourke, "Down on the Farm with Amy Grant," *Today's Christian Woman* (Sept./Oct. 1990): 47.

put us through his sieve of mental, spiritual, and physical affliction to see how we stand up to real trouble. He wants, in the end, to prove we'll fail. He did this with Peter and Job.

Sowing tares (Matt. 13:38-39; 1 John 2:18-19). Satan constantly infiltrates the communities where believers serve and thrive. He plants his "tares"—false "believers" who make a pretense of faith—and uses them to tear down the work of God.

Spreading false doctrine (2 Peter 2:1-3). A big part of Satan's program is the dissemination and cultivation of a body of falsehood that will lead people into error and damnation. He doesn't care much how his disciples twist the truth, so long as it's rendered ineffective.

Inciting persecutions (Rev. 2:10). Satan's work of hindering and thwarting can stoke the flames of persecution. The early church experienced this constantly. Many Christians throughout the world face it daily.

Devouring (1 Peter 5:8). The word means to "drink down," "consume," or "destroy." Satan is not merely content to entrench a believer in sin; he prefers to devour him so that he not only owns God's child but has literally swallowed him up in himself. It's the exact opposite of what God desires to do in us, which, in dwelling within us, makes us freer than ever before.

Seeking opportunities against us (Job 1–2; Luke 22:31-34). A long line of demons continually present petitions to God. "We demand permission to sift Joe like wheat." "We demand permission to attack Betty." "We demand that You take down Your hedge from around Herkimer."

How does this all relate specifically to temptation? Satan's purpose does not end with merely tempting us and making us fall. His real desire is to destroy, hamper, and mock the kingdom of God. His real adversary is God, and we're just the hostages he's taken to try to get at the Almighty.

My daughter watches a movie now and then called *The Little Mermaid.* It's a wonderful example of what movie studios can do that's wholesome, decent, and interesting. In the movie, the Little Mermaid, Ariel, falls in love with a human prince. To become human herself, she makes a pact with the Sea Witch, Ursula. The witch's desire is to add Ariel to her collection of shriveled souls she's cheated over the years and keeps in her miserable garden. But Ursula reveals early on that her real goal is not to keep Ariel; it's to harm her father, King Triton. Toward the end of the movie, the Sea Witch temporarily defeats Triton through her claims on Ariel.

It's the same story with us. We use pawns to get at our real enemies, and in the battle between Satan and God, Satan employs us as mere pawns. What about God? He is neither ruthless nor malignant. He makes us sons and daughters, heirs of His kingdom, and places us into battle as His royal knights.

THE WORLD

Still, our struggle doesn't end with the devil. Our second foe is the world. How does the world figure in the scheme? According to 1 John 2:15-16, there are three ways in which the world appeals to our old nature: through the lust of the flesh, the lust of the eyes, and the boastful pride of life. What are these things?

The "lust" or desire of the flesh takes the normal God-given desire to feel good and perverts it. It begins with our most basic needs — our divinely implanted need for food, sex, sleep, relaxation, leisure, and security. The world takes these normal, healthy, and God-ordained requirements and twists them. It either exaggerates the normal desire, or it tells us to meet the need through illicit means. A whole chorus of sins might be listed: gluttony, laziness, immorality, impurity, sensuality, lack of self-control, love of pleasure, lack of discipline, fornication, drunkenness, drug use, carousing, revelry, unreliability. What are the results? A self-centered, self-absorbed, completely self-oriented person who thinks about nothing but satisfying himself immediately, at whatever cost.

Neither Satan nor the world can invent any new desire. God gave us all our original desires, emotions, and abilities to think and feel. All the world can do is pervert what God has made. In our rebellion against Him, we often do all we can to turn every natural need into a pornographic portrait of lust, selfishness, and deceit.

Many Christian men I've interviewed, especially in preparation for this book, place "sexual lust" at the top of their list of most frequent and difficult temptations. I asked myself why, and the answer became all too obvious. A quick glance at our world tells the story. Everywhere you go, our society displays pictures, products, and people who appeal to that very lust. A man can't go anywhere without being confronted by a horde of women dressed to excite lust.

It's the same thing with food. A horn of plenty crowds our vision, from soda machines in the lunchroom to the dining-out extravaganzas advertised in the paper. It's small wonder we aren't far fatter than we are.

The Bible is replete with people who succumbed to the lust of the flesh. David and Bathsheba are prime examples, but there's also Samson's fornication with Delilah, Noah's drunkenness after the Flood, the debauchery of the sons of Eli, and Solomon's thousands of concubines.

The lust of the eyes takes the normal desire to have beautiful things and perverts it. We see something beautiful or powerful or expensive, and we simply want to possess it. When Achan found the silver and the mantle in the ruins of Jericho, he succumbed to the lust of his eyes and stole them. When King Ahab lusted after Naboth's vineyard and eventually ordered the man killed in order to possess it, he gave in to the lust of eyes. Solomon's greed, Judas Iscariot's outrage at Mary's gift of perfume to Jesus, and Zaccheus' tax thefts all revealed their covetousness.

The lust of the eyes dwells on personal desires and wants beyond actual need. It seeks to possess things, people, places, situations. Its pet sins are covetousness, materialism, ingratitude, greed, hoarding, impatience, unkindness, general nastiness.

It starts when we're little and works its way into every aspect of life. I heard a little girl telling her daddy, "I want this, and I want this, and I want this." After she was done, having pointed out about 400 things, she concluded sincerely, "That's really all I want, Daddy."

The wife tells her husband she must have a mink or she'll die. The businessman wants to clinch that next deal and he'll be happy. The old millionaire believes he'll be content if he can just acquire the Van Gogh at Sotheby's next week.

We think that these things satisfy, but the lust of the eyes is lust. Its rallying cry is "I want." And its cheer is, "More, more, more." But because it's a lust, it can never be satisfied; it only grows into a gobbling monster that consumes all it can and then screams for a little bit more.

The boastful pride of life takes the normal desire to be someone significant and perverts it. It tells a person, "You deserve this." But because basic needs have often been met, it moves on to wishes and hopes. It appeals to the desire for prestige, popularity, power, privilege, and possessions. Its resulting sins are anger, hatred, jealousy, envy, boasting, blasphemy, disobedience, lack of forgiveness, gossip, slander, murder, contention, and selfish ambition. It leads to despair, lack of peace, and an absence of joy in life.

The boastful pride of life afflicted King Saul when he felt challenged by David. King Hezekiah gave into it when he showed the emissaries of Babylon his treasure rooms. Cain also succumbed to it and killed Abel in response. Judas Iscariot perhaps is the most notorious example, having let his jealousy lead him to betray Jesus.

But it's not beyond any of us. I read a cute story some time ago about some workers who laid a twelve-foot section of cement in a sidewalk. Knowing the propensity of dogs and children to leave their mark on such things, the men placed sawhorses around it, thinking this would turn them away. As they both sat down in the shade to have a glass of water, they watched an elderly woman walk by and inspect the sidewalk and then the barrier. They were astonished to see her climb over the sawhorses and write something on the entire length of concrete with the tip of her umbrella. After she left, they walked over and read, "Edna Mae Was Here!"[2]

The devil takes these pleasures of the world and flings them in our faces so that our flesh tingles. If we refuse to listen to our conscience, God's Law, the new nature, or any of our other resources, we'll give in.

THE FLESH

What is the flesh? It's the "old nature," the "old man" that rebels against God. It wants to go its own way, do its own

---

[2]*Reader's Digest,* August 1982.

thing, satisfy its wants in whatever ways it chooses. It wants to do all this without interference from anyone — God, man, minister, Bible, whatever.

The Scripture says that the flesh can know what's right, but it will choose to do what's wrong (Rom. 7:18-19). It becomes excited by the visions the world gives it (James 1:13-15). The law stirs up the flesh so that it fights against the truth (Rom. 7:7-8) and it hates God (8:6-8).

While we might like to think that Satan is responsible for getting us into much sin, James disagrees. He says that when each one "is tempted when, by his own evil desire, he is dragged away and enticed. Then, after desire has conceived, it gives birth to sin, and sin, when it is full-grown, gives birth to death" (James 1:14-15).

Satan doesn't even figure in James' scheme. Why? Because James is emphasizing our responsibility. We can't shift it to Satan and blame him. We have our own illicit desires, ones like the little boy who pushed his friend in the creek, then spit in his face. When his mother confronted him about it, she said, "Did the devil get you to do that?" The boy answered, "Well, pushing him in the creek was the devil's idea, but I thought up spitting in his face all on my own."

THREE GREAT TRUTHS

As powerful as the devil, the world, and the flesh are, we should remember the power of Scripture. God says:

> Of the devil: "The One who is in you is greater than the one who is in the world" (1 John 4:4).
> Of the world: "The world and its desires pass away" (1 John 2:17).
> Of the flesh: "Live by the Spirit, and you will not gratify the desires of the sinful nature" (Gal. 5:16).

No one need live in defeat because of these all-too-present realities. God can show us the way to victory. We can win over all three, because victory is a choice imparted to us by the power of the Spirit.

BATTLE BEGINS

SATAN COMES SLY AND SILVERY

CHAPTER 5

Whatever you do, don't go in that room!"
Ever heard those words? Remember the old movies you saw as a child where the bad guy comes out and entices the hero with the words, "Whatever you do, don't go in there?"

What does the hero proceed to do? Go in. Everyone in the audience is shouting, "Don't go in! Don't go in!" But he opens the door, and the monster latches his teeth into the neck of the poor fool we tried to stop.

Why do we do this to ourselves?

There's an old story about a black slave named Moses who was working in the cotton fields before the Civil War. It was hot, humid, and the rough, thorny cotton had torn his hands. Moses grumbled under his breath, "Dat ole Adam. If not for dat ole Adam."

His master heard him and asked him what he meant.

"It's dat ole Adam dat got us into dis mess. If not for him, I wouldna have to work out in dis here heat."

The master laughed. "So you think you would have done better?"

"You betcha," said Moses.

"All right," said his master. He took Moses into a special house on the plantation and set him up with every expensive convenience. It was wonderful. But there was one problem. The master showed Moses a big black box. "You can live in here and do as you please for as long as you want," he said. "But if you open this box, something bad will happen. Whatever you do, don't open this box."

"Nothin' to it," said Moses.

He went along for several days. Everything he could eat. All the charms of high-class culture. Beautiful beds and chairs. The perfect place for relaxation.

But as time wore on, that black box began to irk him. What was inside that thing that was so bad? Couldn't he take just a little peek?

His mind worked it over and over. But he couldn't figure it out. Finally, he gave in. He went to the box and turned it over in his hands. Then he opened it.

The moment he did a bell rang and the master appeared. "Sorry, Moses. You're no different from that old Adam. He ate the forbidden fruit. You opened the forbidden box. Back to the fields you go."

What is it about that forbidden something that draws us?

That is how it all happened, isn't it? God forbade Adam to eat the fruit of the tree of the knowledge of good and evil. Eve ate. Adam followed. Mankind fell. Ever since we've been reaping the results of that first bite in the Garden.

THE FORBIDDEN FRUIT

Temptation in some ways is like that. Part of its intrigue is the lure of the forbidden. We may not understand why something is forbidden. But the fact that it is rankles us—even ignites our curiosity. Somehow the fact that God says no makes us want to say yes to temptation.

The first temptation found in Scripture offers us some important insights. Before we learn from Jesus, perhaps we need to study ourselves to see how we got into this mess in the first place.

There are only two episodes in Scripture where Satan directly tempts a person: the situation in Genesis 3 with Eve; and the one found in Matthew 4:1-11 and Luke 4:1-13 where Satan confronted Jesus Himself. One story ends in disaster. The other ends with a triumph. As we study the problem of temptation in these pages, we must begin at the same point that God began, with ourselves and our own failure. In that passage lies the key not only to understanding ourselves, but also to victory over Satan in the future.

A LITERAL ADAM AND EVE?

Genesis 3:1-7 records the fall of mankind. For many years, the story has been scoffed at, ridiculed, and derided. One of my college professors used to tell his class, "Anyone who believes the Book of Genesis is either an idiot or the son of one. Take your pick." He used his lightning wit to sear any saint who might take a different view.

How should Christians take the story of Adam and Eve and the Fall? With a snicker? An embarrassed silence? A diffident skepticism? Unquestioning faith?

None of the above. I'm convinced the only posture a committed Christian can take is what I'd call enlightened, thoughtful conviction. By that, I mean belief that is based on the inner enlightening of the Spirit *and* convictions based on clearheaded study of the Word as well as anything that touches on it, including the so-called findings of modern science.

This is not the place for a frontal assault on the theory of evolution. However, let me offer you several reasons why I believe we should take Adam and Eve—their existence, fall, and subsequent redemption—both literally and positively.

First, the Bible presents the existence of Adam and Eve as fact. C.S. Lewis said that anyone who has studied mythology knows that Genesis does not read like a typical myth. It's much more like an account of yesterday's news. It's a spare, uncomplicated rendering of what happened. No emotion. No strains for tears. Just the facts, ma'am. If we are to read the Bible as it was written (and thus intended to be read), we have to accept what the writers wrote, not what we would have wanted them to write. We must accept the fact that they wrote what they believed was historical truth.

Second, we believe in Adam and Eve as our first parents because Jesus and the apostles accepted them that way. Luke presents Adam as the physical ancestor of Jesus (Luke 3:38). Paul refers to him as a historical figure (Rom. 5:14; 1 Cor. 15:22, 45). Jude bases specific doctrines of Scripture on Adam's and Eve's response to Satan in the Garden (1 Tim. 2:13-14). Jude refers to Enoch as being seven generations after Adam (Jude 14). And Jesus built His teaching on divorce not only on the historical facts about Adam and Eve, but also the precise words written in Genesis (Matt. 19:3-6). If Jesus (being God incarnate and therefore the Creator in human flesh) and these other men knew the story was false (and how couldn't they, being filled with and controlled by Jesus' Spirit, who is eternal), then why did they present it as true? If Genesis is false, they become little more than liars who used myths for their own ends.

Third, we believe in Adam and Eve because we have faith, a gift of God. Hebrews 11:3 says, "By faith we understand that the universe was formed at God's command, so that what is seen was not made out of what is visible." The following verse in that chapter refers to the specific sons of Adam and Eve, Cain and Abel. The Christian believes in the Bible's rendering of Adam and Eve not because he knows more science than the scientists, but because God has given him the gift of faith. Through faith we see things that are unseen by others. Through faith we know what is unknown. It's like a sixth sense. By faith we can know and experience realities a person without faith can never know.

Faith can be compared to a television. With a television, anyone can pick up and watch the broadcasts of multitudes of TV stations. But if someone lacks a television with an antenna or cable, he might not even know those broadcasts exist.

Faith is the sensory equipment by which we perceive and receive messages from God through Scripture. With it we apprehend the truths about God and Creation. The enemies of God try to jam those broadcasts of truth. But the true disciple hears His voice and will ultimately—if he seeks to obey God—listen to the truth and accept it.

That's not to say all science is wrong. But I'm convinced that the reason many scientists believe in evolution (there are also many who don't who aren't even Christians) is because they have to explain Creation in some way. If they accept the truths of the Bible, they'll ultimately have to face the God of the Bible. But if they find some other theory that they can use to explain away the Bible, that will satisfy them. Then they don't have to reckon with the God who is holy and true. Thomas Huxley, a nineteenth-century proponent of Darwin's evolutionary theory and an opponent of Christianity, said that he believed in evolution because the alternative conflicted with his lack of morality.

Fourth, the truths about Adam and Eve are the only realistic way to explain the situation our planet is in. The theory of evolution cannot explain morality, right and wrong, or why man seems prone to evil. In fact, according to evolution, mankind should be getting better and better. But reality tells us that's not true. If man is getting better, how is it that the twentieth century has been by far the bloodiest in human history?

It comes down to a decision of faith, a decision both the evolutionary scientist and the Christian have to make. Suppose two men come upon a garden in the middle of a desert. One is a scientist, the other is a theologian. The scientist opens his pack and pulls out a number of instruments. He examines the soil and finds a fossil. After several hours of study, he comes to the conclusion that the garden evolved, based on the existence of the fossil he found.

The theologian, on the other hand, does his own excavation. He finds some documents that look authentic. In them they tell about a king who created the garden for man's pleasure. The king is described in detail, and he even offers several rules about the garden to those who would use it.

When the theologian shows the scientist the book, he retorts, "Someone made it up and left it here. It's a myth. I trust my instruments."

What I'm trying to illustrate is this: both men believe what they believe on the basis of certain facts they accept. But they accept those facts by faith. They can't prove their beliefs unless the king appears. And even if he does, the scientist might just say, "He's an impostor!" That is, until the king throws the scientist into his dungeon!

The scientist who believes in evolution does so on the basis of faith in instruments, studies, reports, and experiments. What he lacks is eyewitness testimony to validate the process of evolution. He can never *prove* his theory by either scientific or legal means. So he ends up believing it all by faith, just as the Christian takes Creation by faith. For that reason, a Christian need offer no apology for a personal belief in the historical Adam and Eve.

What is important for us at this juncture is the temptation that led to Adam and Eve's fall. Through it we learn several of those important truths so critical to overcoming temptation and living a godly life in this world.

SATAN'S APPROACH

Temptations come to us through various means. Sometimes it's something we hear, see, smell, or touch that excites that first glimmer of desire. At other times, it's a thought that occurs to us. As we turn the thought over and over in our minds, a longing ignites, and we decide to take sinful action. Still other times a person approaches us and entices us with something we know is improper. He presents arguments, offers proofs of enjoyment, coaxes us, or even shames us into committing sin. Satan has a thousand variations on the theme. He can come in guises so appealing that we are taken in simply by his apparent sincerity.

That is one of the mystifying things about the world we live in. When Adam and Eve fell, we were subjected to a being so tricky and cunning that none of us could ever defeat him on our own. Ultimately, God Himself had to enter our realm in the person of Jesus and destroy our enemy for us.

How then did Satan approach Eve?

He used an appealing, attractive guise. The text says, "Now the serpent was more crafty than any beast of the field" (Gen. 3:1). That the serpent was possessed by Satan is clear from the context, but also from passages like Revelation 12:9 and 20:2, which make direct reference to their collaboration. What was this serpent?

The word for serpent means "shining" or "glowing." Being a "beast of the field," it was probably a four-footed animal (it became like a snake, crawling on its belly, after God's curse in Gen. 3:14). But it was also more "crafty" than any other beast. That word in this context does not mean cunning or shrewd, but "graceful and beautiful." Undoubtedly, it possessed tremendous personal appeal. It's possible that it could even talk in some way, since Eve does not seem at all stunned when the serpent spoke. Moreover, the serpent may have been a special companion to Adam and Eve. That seems especially possible considering the conversation Eve had with it. It's natural, unforced, and friendly.

Here is a principle of satanic warfare. He does not normally approach us with a frontal assault. Rather, it's with the friendly pat on the shoulder, the winking eye, and the kindly smile. He tempts us with honey rather than vinegar, and he's a professional at using costume and makeup.

He came to the woman. Again, it's a shrewd move. The commands about the tree were not spoken directly to Eve (Gen. 2:16-17). She received them through Adam. Satan knew the way to get Adam was to confront him at a weak point. His love and commitment to Eve would be just such a point.

Satan always uses strategy in his approach to snare a Christian. Before he ever tries to fell someone, he determines what is the best and simplest way to trip them. Remember, he doesn't have all the time in the world.

While reading a book by an author I tend to revere, I was stunned when he spoke inadvertently of the problem of contemporary rock music, a problem I was coincidentally wrestling with. He argued about it in such a way that it made me feel it was all right to listen to such music. I inferred that my rejection of some of it might be sheer legalism. I'm not sure who was right in the matter, but suddenly I became much more open to doing something I had been fighting off for years. It's possible the powers of darkness were using that author to get at me. I wouldn't have been vulnerable had it been the words of someone I didn't admire.

He came when she was alone. We're most vulnerable to attack when we're alone. Two or three bound sticks never break as easily as one. Satan approached Eve while she was off on her own. She had no one else there to argue with or who could set her straight before she did something irrevocable. She could only rely on what her own senses told her at that moment.

We're not invulnerable to temptation in a crowd. But this story shows one reason why fellowship in the body of Christ is so critical. We need the interaction and example of other believers to help us keep on the narrow path. Franklin P. Jones was quoted in *Reader's Digest* as saying, "Nothing makes it easier to resist temptation than a proper upbringing, a sound set of values — and witnesses."

He asked a question. The first thing Satan did after coming to Eve was ask a simple question. "Indeed, has God said, 'You shall not eat from any tree of the Garden'?"

It stuns me how powerful this ploy was. For one thing, it put Eve in the position of being a helper, an informer. It appealed to her pride and made her think the serpent needed some information that she had. This trick also disarmed her. It made her think the serpent was there just for a friendly little chat. She should have been a bit more wary, especially about anything that related to the tree.

But worst of all, Satan was pulling a classic "playing dead" ploy. Remember those scenes in the old movies where the Indian plays dead, then when the soldier bends over to check, the Indian grabs him and knifes him in the belly? This strategy works not only in movies, but also with temptations. If you can make your victim think you're dead, in need, helpless, you make him completely vulnerable.

He focused her attention on the forbidden. That question did something else: it made Eve eager to correct the serpent, to tell him it was not so. But in so doing, it turned her away from thinking about all the trees she could eat of to the one she couldn't. He began the assault on her curiosity, readying her for the full blow. He confused her. A pastor used to tell me about temptation, "Any time you feel pushed or confused, it's probably the devil doing the talking."

More important, Satan was making God look both bossy and cheap. He approached Eve in a slightly aghast manner. "Good grief, won't God let you eat from any of these trees? Horrors!"

It put her on the defensive, right where Satan wanted her. Satan can outargue anyone human and many angels also. I like what Michael said when he disputed with Satan about the body of Moses in Jude 9. He didn't try to present a logical case for what he was doing. He simply said, "The Lord rebuke you!"

Martin Luther was once so angry at the devil, he threw a vial of ink at him. (You can still see the blotch on his study wall.) In his *Table Talk,* he even advised his students not to argue with the devil, but simply to "break wind" in his face. That may be a little crude, but Luther was serious. The devil loves an argument.

Satan studied Eve's behavior. The most important result of Satan's approach was the opportunity it gave him to study Eve, to find out how much she knew, what she was thinking. He was searching for her point of vulnerability.

I recently read a book about business relations, namely, how to negotiate, sell, and win in the business place. One of the author's points was about talking and listening. He said that all negotiators should learn to be silent. Why? Because it creates a tension in the others present and makes them want to talk. The more they talk, the more they reveal about themselves, their position, their strategy. You let the other guy talk and so find out his weak point.

I used to be amazed at how much time football coaches make their team spend watching movies of previous games of the next weekend's opponent. It's key to winning. You can only take your opponent apart if you know where he has a weak point, an Achilles' heel. By watching those films, the players begin to see where the defensive holes are, who is playing poorly, and who can be counted on to make a mistake.

Likewise, the devil is a master observer. He studies us to find every possible point of attack. If he does not know where to begin, he simply strolls up and asks a question, gets us talking, and then calmly leads us down his path.

Take inventory. What approaches have you seen which have made you vulnerable to temptation?

—You pass by a magazine stand in the drug store, and a photo of a beautiful and nearly naked woman grabs your eyes. You find yourself pausing, then flinching and telling yourself, "Don't look at it." But something within you is shouting, "Go ahead, take a second look. It won't hurt."

—You're filling out your weekly expense report and realize one of your entries might not be legitimate. You think about it, and one of God's commandments comes to mind: "You shall not steal." But then another voice says, "Come on, they're not going to make bones about that one."

—You and your wife discuss seeing a certain movie. It's rated "R" and you don't think you should go. But then you notice a review in the newspaper. The reviewer says, "This picture is the must see of the year. If you miss everything else, don't miss this one. The director has created a master-piece." You're intrigued, drawn. Should you go?

—The pastor calls up and asks you to fill in that Saturday for a certain women's class. You feel a surge of excitement; it's a good opportunity for service. So you say yes. After he hangs up, though, you get another call from a friend who is having a special party at the same time. You start to say no, you have a conflict, but something inside whispers, "It may be a good chance to witness. And the pastor can really get someone else very easily." How do you handle it?

When these kinds of things really happen, they can strike fear and terror in the soul of someone who doesn't know what to do. You can give in to sin before you've even had a chance to think.

Clearly, Satan is a determined adversary. We see in the first few verses of Genesis 3 that he is cunning, appealing, and observant. He knows precisely what he's doing. For that reason, we must know what we're doing, or we'll be done in.

EVE THROWS OUT
THE BOOK

CHAPTER 6

While Satan's approach was sly and smartly choreographed, Eve's answer borders on the sloppy and stupid. Notice what she says: "We may eat fruit from the trees of the Garden, but God did say, 'You must not eat fruit from the tree that is in the middle of the Garden, and you must not touch it; or you will die' " (Gen. 3:2-3).

Stop and consider several things. First, how does Eve's statement sound?

To my reading, it sounds like someone parroting a command. In other words, a little switch in her mind flipped to the page that said, "Concerning the tree," and she read off the command without it passing through her heart or thought processes. In effect, she didn't understand God's command at all. When Satan posed his question, it was obvious to him that she didn't know the meaning or purpose of the command. In fact, she didn't even know the command (but we'll look at that in a moment).

Why didn't Eve understand the command? Because she

didn't think about it, meditate on it, dig into it to lay bare its meaning. What questions should she have asked? Things like:

1. How does the tree impart knowledge of good and evil?
2. What is good and evil?
3. Why was this one tree different?
4. Why did God issue the command in the first place?
5. What is death? What happens when it occurs?

She could have made a list of a hundred such questions, then discussed them with Adam, or better yet, gone to the Lord and posed them to Him. But she didn't. Why?

Laziness. Indifference. Preoccupation with "more important" things. Fear. Perhaps when she asked Adam about the tree, if she did, he replied with something like, "Look, just don't eat it, all right? Don't look at it. Don't touch it. Let's not mess up this thing." Adam might have avoided all discussion, perhaps because he was afraid to admit he also didn't understand it.

But what was it that God wanted them to do? To understand His commands. To come to Him and discuss all those things. To learn about good and evil from His perspective.

Mark this: whenever you learn facts from Scripture without understanding the truths behind them, you become Satan's perfect target, because you'll follow those commands without genuine faith or understanding. Sooner or later he'll convince you of the foolishness of the command.

I remember reading about a college girl who was struggling with her convictions about sex. She finally gave in, saying, "I just couldn't think in terms of 'Mom says no' anymore."

I'm not saying mere meditation on the Word overcomes all temptations. but we must understand not only what we believe, but why. Otherwise, we cannot "set apart Christ as Lord" in our hearts and "make a defense to everyone who asks you to give an account for the hope that is in you, yet with gentleness and reverence" (1 Peter 3:15). Peter was arguing for a thinking faith, not a mindless obedience to commands.

I always think of the story of the young wife who was having difficulty with discipline in her use of money. She spent everything she had on clothing. Her husband finally told her that when the devil tempted her she should quote Scripture.

"What Scripture?" she asked.

"The same one Jesus said to Peter. 'Get thee behind Me, Satan.' "

A week later, she came home with a new batch of clothing. Her husband was furious. "Didn't you quote the Scripture?" he asked.

"I sure did," she said. "When I put on that dress, the devil said to me, 'It looks beautiful, darling.' So I said to him, 'Get thee behind me, Satan.' And he went behind me and said, 'It looks great from over here too.' "

That's a comical sidelight on an important issue. You can't simply parrot Scripture. You have to know it, believe it, and apply it in context.

The moment Eve spoke, Satan's intelligence operation was confirmed. He knew one place where she was weak: she didn't understand God's command. If she didn't understand it, he was sure he could probably convince her that it was not true.

Second question: how close was Eve's answer to God's original statement?

Notice how Eve deviated from God's command.

1. She weakened it. God had said, "From any tree of the Garden you may eat freely" (Gen. 2:16). But Eve said, "From the fruit of the trees of the Garden we may eat." There's quite a difference. She left out "any" and "freely." In effect, she weakened the freedom of God's command. She made it seem smaller, less significant.

We do this often with Scripture. We mitigate the greatness of God's truth with all sorts of little touches. As a result we destroy the beauty of God's universe and turn it from a place of plenty and enjoyment to a place of poverty and infringement. For instance, do you have the idea that worship and prayer are done only in a certain place? That's not God's intent. We can talk to Him anywhere, anytime. But we often lessen God's truth with variations that ultimately weaken our relationship with Him.

2. She changed it. Again, God said, "From the tree of the knowledge of good and evil." But Eve changed it to say,

"From the fruit of the tree that is in the middle of the Garden." Incredible. With one phrase she wiped out the whole significance and meaning of the tree. It was just "the tree in the middle of the Garden" to her. God had intended that she understand great things through this tree, but all she could attach to it was a location.

Again, have you ever changed a command or teaching of Scripture? "Judge not lest you be judged" becomes "never make any judgments at all of anyone." Is that the meaning of the Scripture? Not at all.

How about "in everything give thanks"? We change that to mean "for everything give thanks" and come away thinking God must be a virtual sadist. Give thanks for rape, for murder, for war? No way!

3. She added to God's command. She added, "You shall not touch it." God never said that. Here's the first instance of legalism on record. What did that comment do? It made her afraid of the tree. It made her flee from it rather than confront it and plumb its meaning. Soon the command to her would be, "Don't go near it. Don't look at it. Don't think about it." God had no such purpose in mind.

Christians are always adding to God's commands. Concerning food, we're told that "everything God created is good, and nothing is to be rejected if it is received with thanksgiving" (1 Tim. 4:4). But some groups forbid certain foods such as coffee, tea, soft drinks, pork, junk foods, and wine. People have added to God's commands and come up with all sorts of legalisms on subjects God never spoke on, or would. We turn His gracious gifts into reasons to judge one another.

4. She subtracted from God's command. God had said, "For in the day that you eat from it you shall surely die." The word "surely" is emphatic. You shall "absolutely without pause or question" die.

But what did Eve say? "You must not eat fruit from the tree . . . and you must not touch it, or you will die." She left out, "in the day you eat from it," and "surely." It's a gross subtraction. It makes the command sound weak, unconvincing, a threat without teeth. Later, it would be much easier to ignore such a flimsy command.

In effect, Eve had three problems:

She didn't know God's command.

She didn't understand God's command.

Therefore, she couldn't accurately apply God's command to the situation at hand.

None of this was lost on Satan. He knew immediately that he was dealing with a careless believer who had a half-baked understanding of God. More important, he knew Eve wasn't prepared for dealing with a test about the tree. Whenever God gives us a command in Scripture, you can be sure that Satan will test our willingness to obey. When God issued the command to Adam, the man should have realized that he was going to be tested. However, what's most obvious is that neither Adam nor Eve did anything about the tree. They simply ignored it, perhaps even hoping it would go away.

That's exactly what Satan wants us to do with biblical truth. Then when he drops by to test our willingness to obey, he knows he has an unprepared victim.

An ace pitcher in the National League was asked the secret of his success. He pulled out a little black notebook. In it he kept detailed notes on every batter he'd ever faced or saw someone else face. He quickly learned the weak points of every batter in the league. When a hitter stood up to face him, he knew precisely how to pitch to that man's weakness.

You can be sure Satan will test you not only at your weak points, but at any point which God considers important. For Adam and Eve, understanding the tree of the knowledge of good and evil was the most important issue in their lives. They should have studied the matter, thought it through, anticipated every possible point of attack, and been ready. But they didn't. And they weren't.

You might say, "Hey, Littleton, they were new at this. They were totally innocent. They didn't know they had an enemy."

True. But both should have recognized the importance of the tree. The moment it was mentioned, a reverence should have filled their minds. Instead, what you see in Eve is a totally lax attitude. "Oh, that tree? Aw, we're not supposed to eat it or touch it, lest we die. Nothin' big about that one."

Satan loves such an outlook. He drags the victims home every time.

Moving on to our third question: how much do you think it matters that Eve may have made a few mental errors? Do you think it matters at all?

If we use the Lord Jesus as our primary example, we can turn to Matthew 4:1-11 and see how He used Scripture in His confrontation with Satan. In each case, He quoted the Book of Deuteronomy accurately, appropriately, and with an understanding of the meaning and context. He defeated Satan because He knew how to use Scripture.

But Eve didn't.

The Lord has instructed us that letter-perfect knowledge of His Word is critical to victory over temptation. "I have hidden Your Word in my heart that I might not sin against You" (Ps. 119:11). The word for "hidden" means "to value and place in a secure and safe place." To "prize" it. To "reverence" it.

Is that how you treat God's Word? If you're sloppy and don't take time to memorize it word by word, you'll be an easy mark for the devil. You can't apply properly what you don't know perfectly.

Another verse is helpful: "Do your best to present yourself to God as one approved, as a workman who does not need to be ashamed, and who correctly handles the word of truth" (2 Tim. 2:15). Sometimes people use this in reference to a pastor's study in preparation for his messages. But it applies to all Christians who study God's Word, and certainly to anyone who will teach others. Paul argues for such things as (1) diligence—a rigorous determination to accomplish one's mission; (2) approval by God—a concern to please Him above all; (3) workmanship—one who works in the trenches, a common laborer who does the hard work that few are willing to do; (4) not being ashamed—for we shall stand before Him in judgment; and (5) accurate handling of the Word. God wants us to be absolutely clear about His Word: we must not toy with it. It's the most sacred treasure we have in this world.

Eve was in deep trouble. Satan's one question had led her to reply in such a way that her ignorance and laziness became apparent. She was toying with God's command. She had no understanding of the seriousness of what was happening because she hadn't taken God's word seriously.

We have to ask ourselves: How much am I like Eve?

EVE BITES THE APPLE AND THEY BOTH BITE THE DUST

CHAPTER 7

The moment Eve answered Satan, he unleashed his full attack. He had no fear that he would be contradicted or put in his place. As a result, the first thing he did was tell a bold, unflinching lie: "You surely shall not die." He used the same words God used earlier to say, "You surely shall die," except he puts a "not" in front of it. The Hebrew expression for "You surely shall die" is so emphatic that it bears mentioning. Literally it means, "Dying you shall die." It's Hebrew's most insistent construction. "This is it, folks. Write it down and post it under the sink, on the kitchen table, and over the mantle. You do this, and you're dead! No ifs, ands, or buts. I'm as serious as I can get!"

Notice four elements of Satan's attack.

HE CONTRADICTED GOD

He told the boldest, fattest, and dirtiest lie in history. What's astonishing is that it was such a direct contradiction of God's own words to Adam. How can anyone be so brazen?

It's easy. When you're dealing with someone who's fuzzy on the truth, you can say anything. Anything! And a person will often swallow it — hook, line, sinker, reel, and rod! They'll even be happy they took it. They'll boast about it. "Man, was I smashed last night, Harry. I mean I was retching my guts out. Haw! Haw!" It always used to amaze me during my high school and college years how people would brag about sin.

Satan is so brazen that when he knows the person he's tempting is ignorant of the truth, he'll even quote God's Word, but with some kind of twist to contradict its meaning.

How often have you found yourself hearing people offer direct contradictions of God's commands and truths? The Word says, "Fornication is wrong." But a friend says, "It's not, it's beautiful. Don't turn God's good gift into a ridiculous rule."

The Word says, "You shall not steal." The world says, "No, everybody fudges a little. You have to. You couldn't survive financially any other way."

The Bible says, "Pray without ceasing." Satan says, "Prayer is for weaklings. Get on with it. Have it your way."

SATAN ACCUSED GOD
OF HAVING WRONG MOTIVES

Have you noticed that when you speak the truth people often accuse you of having wrong motives? "He's just saying that because he thinks he's so much better than us."

"Oh, they all say that stuff because they can't think for themselves."

"Come off it — you don't believe that, do you? You people say those things because you don't know how to have any fun."

Where did it all start? Right at the beginning. Remember what Satan said to God about Job when God asked him if he'd noticed how well he served? "Pooh! Does Job fear God for nothing? Haven't You protected him from everything and blessed every little job he does? No, You strike him down and take away what he has and he'll curse You to Your face" (Job 1:9-11, paraphrase). The devil said that Job had wrong motives. No one serves God because He's worthy, but because of what they get out of Him.

Peter got the same treatment. When Jesus warned the disciples they'd all desert Him, Peter refused to believe it. Then Jesus informed him that Satan had asked to "sift him like wheat" (Luke 22:31). Why? Though the Scripture doesn't say, it's obvious. Satan wanted to show Peter wasn't really committed to Jesus. He wanted to prove he was in it only as long as he got something out of it. But when his life was threatened, he'd cry uncle. And at first, Peter did. But later he would bring honor to God.

Satan doesn't believe anyone does anything for the right motives. Not even God. He told Eve, "For God knows that when you eat of it your eyes will be opened, and you will be like God, knowing good and evil" (Gen. 3:5). In other words, "Get this straight, Eve. The only reason God doesn't want you eating from that tree is because He's afraid you'll become equal to Him."

How many times have you heard that ploy?

"God forbids it because He doesn't want us having fun. He wants to keep all the good things for Himself."

"The Scriptures speak against it because the people of those times weren't as advanced as we are."

Why does Satan ascribe underhanded motives to everyone? Because he knows his own motives. He thinks everyone must be like him. Of course, he'd never admit it to anyone. But isn't that why many of us condemn in others the same things that we do ourselves? We think everyone operates like we do.

Why does Satan attack God by questioning His motives? Because it's the only thing that can't truly be seen. You can never prove motives. Words and actions can be heard and seen. Satan could never condemn God's deeds. So he attacks His motives, because then he could accuse in any way he wanted.

SATAN OFFERED A REWARD FOR DISOBEDIENCE

"Your eyes will be opened and you will be like God, knowing good and evil."

Sin always offers something for us. Something immediate. Something gratifying. Something important. Sin offers a very real and instant payment. To defeat temptation, one of the first things we ought to say to ourselves is, "Is it too easy? Am I getting what I want without any real cost on my part?"

Most of creation's joys come at a price. Salvation even carries the price tag of faith and repentance. Still, that's far more than many are willing to pay. But Satan's offerings are lined up along Easy Street. Payday is later. What matters is now.

SATAN WAITED

Satan also uses the waiting game. Plant an idea, then stop. Wait. Let the victim take it and run. After he lied to Eve, he stopped. He let Eve turn it over in her mind. If she needed some further direction, he'd supply it. But he had to give her time to think, and to think in the wrong way.

EVE'S ACCEPTANCE

From there it's straight down. "When the woman saw that the fruit of the tree was good for food and pleasing to the eye, and also desirable for gaining wisdom, she took some and ate it" (Gen. 3:6).

Some have noted that Eve's three observations compare nicely to the lust of the flesh (it was "good for food"), the lust of the eyes (it was "pleasing to the eye"), and the boastful pride of life ("desirable for gaining wisdom") from 1 John 2:15-16. But what concerns me more is that none of it repeats what Satan said. She doesn't refer at all to her eyes being opened, being like God, or knowing good and evil. She thought only in terms of "being wise." Why is this?

Here is an important truth about the nature of temptation. Rarely does Satan understand what we really want. Certain parts of our hearts and minds are closed to him. But what he does understand is that if he can simply guide a person's thinking, she'll come up with her own reasons for sinning!

The moment we depart from revealed truth (the Word of God) and begin using our innate reasoning and observation, we are in great danger. Everything we choose to believe must rely on revealed truth, or we will go astray.

Think of it. Eve was sinless, but the moment she rejected God's Word, her mind led her in several wrong directions.

Someone might object, "But what you're saying is that Eve

sinned before she ate the fruit." No, because there was only one sin possible at that time in history—physically eating the fruit. Eve could think and do anything—she was totally free—and it was all right in the eyes of God. There was only one command she had to obey.

Remember what Paul said, "Sin is not taken into account when there is no law" (Rom. 5:13). That is, so long as God has not established a law about something, we're free to do as we please. Eve could have reasoned any way she liked. She didn't sin until she actually ate of the tree.

Knowing and obeying God's Word is the critical part of every moment of our lives. The moment we depart from that we're in great danger. Reason that departs from God's Word is false reason.

ADAM'S ACQUIESCENCE

So where does the stalwart husband figure in all this? Eve ate. "She also gave some to her husband, who was with her, and he ate" (Gen. 3:6). That's all it says. No argument. No outrage. No questions. No rebukes. "He ate."

Why?

Paul comments in 1 Timothy 2:14, "And Adam was not the one deceived; it was the woman who was deceived and became a sinner." In other words, Adam was not at all hoodwinked by Satan's lies. He knew they were lies. He knew if he ate he would die. He knew he wouldn't be like God. He knew the fruit wasn't good for food, or a delight to the eyes, or powerful to make one wise. He walked into the disaster with his eyes open.

But why? What possessed the man?

Because he was afraid his wife would reject him?

Because he felt that now that it was done he might as well go along?

Because he was so weak-willed he couldn't stand up to her?

I don't think it was any of the above. There's only one reason I see for Adam's sin: he chose to rebel, knowing full well that it was rebellion, and knowing that he would bring death on the whole race. He simply didn't care. He chose to reject God's way.

Why?

Wasn't Adam perfect, flawless in mind, emotions, and will? Yes.

Didn't Adam realize the pain he would bring on himself and all his children? Probably.

Didn't Adam see that there was a way out, that he didn't have to sin even though Eve was deceived? Maybe.

Why then did he sin?

Adam was exercising his power and right to choose. That's the all-important principle. We all have the power and right to choose to go God's way, or our way. That's the whole story of temptation: the awesome responsibility of free choices. Will you obey God? Or will you choose to disobey? That's why victory is indeed a choice.

I often think of two important choices in Peter's life. The first happened when he denied three times he knew Jesus. In each instance he was tempted, put to a test. What might have gone through his mind? "If I say I know Him, they may kill me." Or, "If I agree that He's my Lord, they may laugh at me." Peter made a choice. He didn't have to deny Jesus. But he did. Sure, he was afraid. Sure, he was pushed. Sure, he was tired and weak and alone. But it came down to a choice. No one forced him to deny he knew Jesus. He chose to deny Him of his own volition.

The second situation arose some fifty-two days later, on the Day of Pentecost. The disciples had gathered to pray and fellowship. They were exhilarated from seeing Jesus alive. Then the Holy Spirit came upon them, rushing like wind, dancing upon their heads in flames of fire, and loosing their tongues with the praises of God. Suddenly, each of them possessed the ability to speak in languages they'd never learned. They bounded into the street and spoke to everyone who passed.

But the crowd was scornful. Some said they were drunk. Others commented that they must be mad. Still others were silently curious. Why was this happening?

I have to wonder what was going on in Peter's mind. Perhaps he had a short conversation with himself. "Someone should tell the people this is the thing Jesus promised, that the prophets spoke about."

"But who?"

"Why not you?"

"Me? I couldn't . . . "

"Yes, you can. Do it. Stand up. Tell them."

"But I've never spoken before so many people. I might not say the right thing."

"God will give you the words."

"But James and John are so much better with words. They can speak."

"No, you should."

"But I'm afraid. They might . . . "

"Laugh?"

"Well, yes."

"Curse you?"

"I don't know. Maybe."

"Hate you?"

"Yes, they might feel that way."

"Kill you?"

"No. I don't think . . . "

"Then speak. Choose today whom you will serve. Peter . . ."

"Or?"

"Jesus."

There's a long pause. Suddenly Peter rises before the crowd. As he does, he whispers, "I choose Jesus." He begins speaking. The crowd is transfixed. When it's all over, 3,000 people believe in Jesus Christ. Do you think Peter ever regretted that choice?

One of my professors used to say, "You can live a life of no regrets." What are regrets? Temptations you gave into. Wrong choices you made in tight situations. It doesn't have to be that way. There is a way to overcome temptation. It's by learning to go God's way, instead of Satan's way, the world's way, or our way. It's a choice. We can choose not to sin. Sometimes choosing not to is the hardest work in the world.

It isn't easy. I admit that up front. But we will discover that there is hope. Where? In Jesus. In Him alone.

Will you choose to run with Him?

Or against Him?

THE BATTLE JOINED

DOES GOD LEAD US INTO TEMPTATION?

CHAPTER 8

Matthew 4:1 makes one of the most remarkable statements found in Scripture: "Then Jesus was led by the Spirit into the desert to be tempted by the devil."

God led Him there? To be tempted? To be put into the hands and wiles of Satan?

That's precisely what it says.

There are other equally befuddling assertions in Scripture. Satan appeared before God in Job 1 and informed the Almighty that if He would simply destroy Job's possessions, that godly man would curse Him to His face. Satan dropped a juicy chunk of bait and God apparently leapt to the platform. "Very well," He says, "then everything he has is in your hands, but on the man himself do not lay a finger" (Job 1:12). God chose not to strike Job Himself, but He did something that looks even more sinister: He put Job into the hands of Satan, with a single restriction: he could not touch Job personally, just his wealth.

In Luke 22:31-34, a passage I've already referred to several times, Jesus tells Peter that he'll deny he even knows Him. His words are, "Simon, Simon, Satan has asked to sift you as wheat. But I have prayed for you, Simon, that your faith may not fail. And when you have turned back, strengthen your brothers." Peter protests that he's willing to go to death rather than let Jesus be taken. Jesus concludes that not only will he fail in that venture, but he'll end up denying he even knows Jesus.

Notice several rather astonishing truths from that passage. First, Satan "asked" to sift Peter. He had to get permission. That's encouraging. Nonetheless, look at what follows: "I have prayed for you that your faith may not fail." Again, a word of assurance. There's still hope. But then the terrifying thought: "when you have turned back." Five words, yet what an astonishing revelation! Jesus is predicting that Peter will fall! After that, he'll repent. But the fact that Jesus seems to give consent to Peter's fall certainly chills our blood. It's reassuring that Peter was reconciled with Jesus. But even to be in Satan's hands temporarily is scary.

Then there's Paul. God sent him a "thorn in the flesh, a messenger of Satan, to torment [him]" (2 Cor. 12:7). Paul pleaded three times for God to take this spirit away. But God refused, telling him His power became perfect in weakness.

That's only slight comfort. What kind of God do we have — One who can be trusted only to lead us into temptation, put us into Satan's hands, and let us be sifted like wheat? Sure, maybe we'll survive. Undoubtedly, He'll see us through. But it's the "through" that troubles us. We've seen enough people who didn't make it "through" to give us pause. What about all those Christians who have given up the faith in the face of terrible trials and temptations? Could we end up like one of those people?

THE LORD'S PRAYER

In the Lord's Prayer, Jesus instructed His disciples to petition God with the words "and lead us not into temptation" (Matt. 6:13). Does that mean He might lead us into temptation if we fail to ask Him? Might He even do the same things to us that He did with Jesus, Peter, Job, and Paul, allowing

Satan to inflict harm on us for a season?

To add to this theological difficulty we have a stern word from James: "When tempted, no one should say, 'God is tempting me.' For God cannot be tempted by evil, nor does He tempt anyone; but each one is tempted when, by his own evil desire, he is dragged away and enticed" (James 1:13-14).

Jesus was "led up by the Spirit into the desert," Job was put into Satan's hands, Peter was sifted like wheat, and yet God remains above it all: He does not tempt anyone. In fact, He can't even be tempted to tempt anyone.

What on earth is going on here?

This is an example of what theologians sometimes call an "antinomy." It's an apparent contradiction between two equally valid principles or truths. For instance, God is one. We are monotheists. Yet, God is also a "tri-unity," existing as three persons. Some theologians have qualified this by saying God is "one essence" but exists in three personas — the Father, the Son, and the Spirit. How can there be one God and yet three Persons who are all equally divine? It's a mystery, an antinomy. Both conditions are true, even though our minds cannot easily reconcile them.

There are a multitude of antinomies in Scripture. Jesus is wholly God and wholly man in one person. The Bible is "God-breathed" and infallible. Yet it was written by men who are fallible. We are saved by grace, a sovereign and God-initiated act; yet, at the same time, when we believe, we are making a free and uncoerced choice as human beings. Moreover, God is utterly sovereign and in complete control over everything that happens in His world. Yet we are responsible for what we do and accountable to Him as if He were not sovereign at all. Man is flesh, lives, dies, and turns to dust, yet he also has an eternal soul.

All these truths are to some degree antinomies. Similarly, the problem of temptation contains several contradictory elements. God can lead Jesus up into the wilderness to be tempted by the devil, yet God is not responsible for the actual tempting. God could put Peter in circumstances where He knew Peter would fail; yet at the same time, God did not cause Peter to fail, nor could Peter blame Him for what happened by saying, "You did it to me! You put me in this situation, knowing I'd fail!" Peter could only crawl off and moan about his sin.

In some ways it appears unfair. It looks like God pulls the strings while we get blamed for the results. Yet, in other ways one can discover a glorious truth that provides tremendous encouragement to those who will seek to understand it. Just because God knows we'll fail in a situation does not make Him culpable. If a football coach sends in a fullback to run the ball when he knows that fullback isn't strong enough to run through the linebackers, does that make it the coach's fault when the fullback gets tackled? Did the coach force him to be tackled? Did the coach make those linebackers run over his linemen?

No, when that fullback chose to play in the game, he came under that coach's leadership. That coach knows there will be casualties. But the fullback entered the stadium freely, without coercion.

Similarly, when Adam chose to sin in the Garden, he and every other person who would ever live chose that route. He put himself into perilous circumstances. Certainly God allowed Satan to tempt Eve and then Adam. But God also gave them all the equipment and help they needed to pass the test. They chose to fail on their own.

Did God know they would fail ahead of time? Yes. Was that failure part of His eternal plan? Absolutely. But did God make them fail? Did He force them to make the choices they did? No. Therefore, they're responsible.

Similarly, when we choose to become Christians and follow Christ to the point of death, we also choose to trust God about all that comes at us in this life. We believe that He will sovereignly work all events for good in our lives, even bad things, even temptations, failures, blowouts, reversals, and self-destructive acts. That means He will allow us to go through difficult times when everything seems to go wrong. But ultimately He promises to bring matters to a right conclusion. We must trust in that truth and that reality, or there's no point in being a Christian. If I as a believer could not rely on the fact that God promises to see me through, help me up when I'm down, and lead me on to glory, I'd give up this minute. Why struggle if in the end there's no assurance of victory? Why get into the battle if we're not certain it's a winning cause?

What then is God's purpose in allowing us to go through temptation? Why did He lead Jesus up into the wilderness? Why did He allow Job to live through such horrid circumstances? Why did He put Peter in circumstances where He knew the disciple would disown Jesus?

Understanding God's purpose in allowing temptation provides the key to victory. If we know the why of a situation, we can endure any what, when, where, and how.

GOD'S PURPOSES

The primary purpose of temptation, as I revealed earlier, is to produce obedience. Hebrews 5:8 says that Jesus "learned obedience from what He suffered." Earlier in the same book, the writer says, "In bringing many sons to glory, it was fitting that God . . . should make the author of their salvation perfect through suffering" (Heb. 2:10). James told us to "consider it pure joy . . . whenever you face trials of many kinds" (James 1:2). The word for "trials" could just as well be translated "temptations." He goes on to say that "testing of your faith develops perseverance," and that eventually leads us to real maturity.

Paul rejoiced in trials and temptations and made the point that "suffering produces perseverance, perseverance, character, and character, hope" (Rom. 5:3). He also asserted that Jesus became "obedient to death—even death on a cross" (Phil. 2:8). He might have also said He was obedient to the point of starvation (see Matt. 4:1-4), that He chose obedience rather than putting God to the test (vv. 5-7), and that He desired God more than riches (vv. 8-10).

We can only learn to obey by living in and through situations where we have a choice to disobey. That choice is prompted by temptation. Satan entices us to disobey God and go our own route, or even his. If we never had any real moral choices, we'd be little better than robots conditioned and programmed to respond only one way to stimuli. Such a situation denies the integrity, freedom, and glory of man. God will not do that. He chooses to leave His beloved children in perilous circumstances where they will exercise real, robust, and responsible wills rather than leave them in a perfect environment where no moral decisions exist.

I personally believe that even in heaven, even when God's perfect kingdom begins, we will still face moral and spiritual dilemmas. Somehow, though, God insures that we will always have the resources to make the right and God-glorifying choices. He will create that perfect environment, yet it will be done without compromising our humanity. We will be like God—knowing good and evil—and yet able always to choose the good freely, honorably, and joyfully.

Ultimately, we only learn to obey God when we have a real, honest, and specific choice not to. That was part of the reason God tested Adam and Eve in the Garden. We demonstrate our true loyalties when we're tested to the quick. That is, when a temptation arrives on our doorstep which is truly alluring—say a dessert draped in mocha chocolate with toasted coconut on top—and we know we're forbidden this delectable little treat, our willingness to obey becomes all the more apparent. When we learn to obey even "when it hurts," then we've truly learned the lifestyle God wants us to have.

In temptation, God urges dependence on Him. Paul wrote in 2 Corinthians 12:9-10 that God's power was "perfected in weakness" and "when I am weak, then I am strong." Those words appear in the context of Paul's struggle with a thorn in the flesh. We don't know what the thorn was, but it involved pain and perseverance. What was God trying to do through that trial? To teach Paul that the more he depended on God, the more God's power became available to him. If he wasn't weak, he would attempt to do things on his own. As we face temptations that defy our human strength and wisdom, God shouts in our ear, "I sent this so you'd learn to depend on Me, not yourself."

Trials ready us for future work. Jesus "became obedient to the point of death, even death on a cross," says Paul in Philippians 2:8. But before that cataclysmic moment, He'd learned obedience in previous days while being tempted by the devil in the wilderness. Through testing and temptation, God prepared Jesus for His future work. If He couldn't face the little tests of refusing to turn stones into bread and standing up for the truth against the Pharisees, how would He have fared when He met the ultimate test of the Cross? He wouldn't have been ready. Just as a football coach pushes his team to the limit during the week through calisthenics, play making, blocking, tackling, and running to ready them for a game, so God readies us for major temptations by disciplining us on a daily basis.

Trials perfect us. James tells us that the "testing of [our] faith develops perseverance" and that we're to let endurance have its perfect result, "that you may be mature and complete, not lacking anything" (James 1:3-4). God perfects us — matures, develops, establishes, and refines us — through testing and temptation. Perfection is the process of ridding ourselves of every flaw. Of course, God never completes that process in anyone in this world. But He starts it here and chips away daily to rid us of those flaws. While none of us will ever be sinless, it's also true that we are to sin less and less. That's the perfection process. Every one of us entered into it the moment we trusted Christ.

Testing allows us to overcome sins and problems. The only way God can help us overcome a problem is by exposing it, bringing it to light, and helping us design ways to end its power. If we pray for patience, do we think that everything will go perfectly day by day? No, chances are that if we need patience, God will send us circumstances that stretch our patience to its limits. The boxer only becomes more skillful by lifting heavier weights, fighting stronger opponents, and landing harder punches. We learn gentleness, goodness, love, kindness, and everything else by being thrust into rough, evil, unloving, and nasty circumstances that try us to the breaking point. It's there that God is elongating our powers beyond anything they could ever be in a world without problems.

God uses temptation to sharpen us. Proverbs 27:17 says, "Iron sharpens iron; so one man sharpens another." Trials and temptations are the literal whetstone God takes to us to sharpen our character, capacity, and commitment to Him. A blade can be hardened only by putting it through the heat.

Trials expose weaknesses. We've already spoken of this one, but it bears repeating. God allows us to be tempted in certain situations where He knows we will fall to show us where we're weak. Fall once and you've got an opportunity to learn, to get up and find the way of escape. Fall twice, maybe you didn't get the point. Study the problem again. Fall three times, and maybe the problem is you: you're just not willing to face this problem the way you should.

To be sure, all of us have sins and habits which we give in to repeatedly. But if that's the case, we can't excuse our problems. We need to face them all the more earnestly and reckon with our commitment to growth and holiness. I find that the main reason I give in to certain temptations over and over is because I don't really want to win over them enough to expend my greatest effort.

Testing shows the world we're real. In 1 Corinthians 4:9 Paul refers to himself as being a "spectacle to the world, both to angels and to men." He referred especially to his suffering as an apostle. But the same truth applies to all Christians. We are a spectacle to angels and to men. They watch us. They study us. They notice our vices and rejoice in (or grimace at) our virtues. They're constantly on the look-out, seeking an excuse for their own sin through ours, or being convicted of their sin through our obedience to Christ. But regardless of what conclusions they come to, the truth remains that we are God's display pieces. He holds us up as examples of His character, His image, His grace, power, goodness, and love. Victory over temptation is His way of showing us off. Such a truth should both urge us to live boldly and wisely for Him, as well as rebuke our failure to live obediently before Him.

By virtue of our faith, we are examples to the world. We cannot escape it. What kind of examples we are can be summed up with one of two verses of Scripture. The first tells of the person who claims to be a Christian yet fails utterly to obey God. Of this person, Paul said that "the name of God is blasphemed among the Gentiles because of you" (Rom. 2:24). In the other case, Peter encourages the believer to sin less and less and so win the praise of the world. He said, "Live such good lives among the pagans that, though they accuse you of doing wrong, they may see your good deeds and glorify God on the day He visits us" (1 Peter 2:12).

Like it or not, the world measures God by His people. They shouldn't. It's foolish. But that's the way it is. Remarkably, God is not ashamed that we call Him our Father, even though we often fail to live up to any of His commands. Every temptation we face—tonight, tomorrow, and the next day—is an opportunity to show that we are His and that He is worthy of our obedience. That is ultimately the question in every temptation: Will I obey Him, or myself?

DOES GOD EVER WANT US TO FAIL?

Even though we understand God's purposes in temptation, we might still wonder: Does God ever actually "want" us to fail? Jesus knew Peter's loyalty would fail. God knew Job would be transformed from a loving disciple to a complaining cynic. He also saw that Jesus didn't succumb to Satan's taunts in Matthew 4. But did God want Peter and Job to fail in the ways they did?

It's important to grasp the difference between God's "feelings," "wants," "desires," and "preferences," and His sovereign choices and plan. In one sense, to say that God has desires or preferences seems almost ludicrous. How could He who is all-powerful "desire" something and not get it?

Well, He does! Take a look at 1 Timothy 2:4: He "wants all men to be saved and to come to a knowledge of the truth." Are "all" men saved? Have "all" come to the knowledge of the truth? Of course not. But clearly, God has a desire that they be saved.

Similarly, Ephesians 4:30 states that we can "grieve" the Holy Spirit. Obviously when He feels grief about something, He must have had a "wish" for something else. But that wish was denied.

In the same way, I believe God can "wish" or "desire" one thing and yet His sovereign plan requires something far different. God "wants" all men to be saved. However, His eternal plan has decreed that some people will end up in hell. Jesus "wanted" to gather Jerusalem under His arms like a mother hen gathers her chicks (Matt. 23:37). But the people of Israel rejected Him, and His plan included that rejection.

What is the result?

First, God's "wants" may be different from what He allows

to happen. He does not want us to fail. But His plan allows for failure. A baseball coach doesn't "want" any of his players to strike out (unless he's a complete sadist). But he knows it will happen and accepts it.

Second, God's plan includes every failure we will ever experience, as well as every victory. Nothing takes God by surprise. Peter's denials didn't faze Jesus. He knew the experience would carry Peter on to greater heights than he could ever have known otherwise.

I like what Joseph said to his brothers in Genesis 50:20, years after they'd sold him into slavery: "You intended to harm me, but God intended it for good to accomplish what is now being done, the saving of many lives." Satan used temptation for evil ends. He longs to destroy us. But God always allows trying circumstances for our good. If we fail, He can turn us around. And if we succeed, He will teach us humility and move us on to greater and richer experiences.

Third, we never have to fail. First Corinthians 10:13 assures us that God always provides a way of escape. He remains faithful. We can trust that when we fail, it's our fault. But it is also true that we never "have" to fail. We cannot face a temptation with the attitude that "this must be one God decreed that I fall to." No, God's command is that we "resist the devil," "draw near to God," and "overcome by the blood of the Lamb." We can never be sure of the outcome of any temptation until it's behind us. But as we go through trials, we face them with the attitude that they can always be overcome. Victory is indeed a choice.

One woman I interviewed for this book told me this story. I'll call her Jenny. Her college-age daughter asked her to take in a homeless man she'd met at church. He had suffered some reverses and needed just a few months to get back to normal. He had a job and attended college, and Jenny liked him. The young man was soon confiding in Jenny like she was his own mother. Often, they both talked late into the night.

Then disaster struck. Jenny began to feel strongly attracted to him in ways she hadn't felt in twenty years toward anyone but her husband. She said, "I felt like a high school girl with a bad crush. His lips, his smile, his physique appealed to me in a very persistent way. I found myself wishing I were a young girl, free to hold his hand and stroll with him through the park."

When she realized what she was feeling, she became alarmed. She felt too embarrassed to tell anyone about it, but she didn't want to tell him to leave without a good reason. She began to pray. She said, "Jesus' words, 'Why sleep ye? Rise and pray, lest ye enter into temptation' became my battle cry. I rose in the middle of the night and prayed fervently for wisdom and self-control. I could hardly stand living in my own house anymore. It was torture to be around him, and I was afraid that I might make a fool of myself and/or ruin the young man."

She stopped her late night counseling with him and got a part-time job. This helped her combat her feelings. But finally she decided to talk to a Christian counselor. "Then," she says, "the very day I made the appointment, God did a miracle. He broke the cycle I was in. Suddenly my special feelings stopped and never came back. I could look at and speak with the young man with no temptation plaguing me."

In conclusion, she said, "I share this story because in our morally loose society temptation is given fertile soil. It's important that people hear Jesus is real and that prayer works. Temptation is strong, but that bond between a Christian and her Savior is stronger. Jesus will never leave us or forsake us."

That's a good word for all of us caught in the turmoil of temptation. Victory is possible. With His help, we can find the way of escape, stand firm, and live above our circumstances. Temptation is never overwhelming. Victory is not only possible but probable when we learn to make the right choices.

TO OBEY OR NOT TO OBEY: THAT IS THE TEMPTATION

CHAPTER 9

Imagine a scenario in which God the Father has informed you that you're not allowed to eat a bite until He says so. While you're twiddling your thumbs, dreaming of Eskimo Bars and filet mignon, the devil sashays up to you and says, "Aw, go ahead, hit the refrigerator. You're hungry, aren't you?"

What kind of replies might you offer in response?

"Well, actually, I'm on this special diet."

"For some reason, God won't let me eat anything."

"I know it probably sounds foolish, but God told me to hold off until He gives the OK. I don't know exactly why, but I think I should stick with Him."

"I really do feel like it, but I think I should hold off. I don't want to make God mad at me."

What happens in such a situation? We all know very well: the devil comes up with extremely intelligent reasons why our line of thought is wrong. Take the first statement. Let's imagine a whole conversation with the devil.

The devil whispers, "Aw, go ahead, hit the refrigerator. You're hungry, aren't you?"

You answer, "Well, actually, I'm on this special diet."

The devil already sees his opportunity. "Get off it. You're not on a diet. God told you not to eat anything."

You hang your head, a little embarrassed. "Yeah, that's true. But I'm sure He has His reasons."

"Reasons, schmeasons! What reasons might He have to tell you not to eat anything for—what is it?—forty days now? That's unconscionable. What kind of loving person would expect that of someone like you?"

You scratch your head. "He is wise, devil. I mean, He must have some good reason for why He's doing this to me."

"Then what is it?"

You clear your throat, eyeing the kitchen with longing. "Uh, He's doing it for my health. That's it!"

"Oh, yeah! Look at you. You're starving. Your muscles have atrophied. In another hour it'll be all over for you, buddy. Look, you're sitting here trying to concentrate on reading your Bible. But you're so hungry you can't think of anything but that microwave pizza in the fridge. Get a bite to eat and then you'll be able to read properly."

"You don't think one bite would hurt?"

"Absolutely not. It'll restore your energy. You'll be able to serve Him so much better. Hey, remember the story of King Saul and Jonathan, how King Saul forbade anyone to eat, and then Jonathan scarfed up some honey he found and fought all the better? Everyone agreed King Saul was being ridiculous. It was a stupid order. How different is this from that?"

"You know, I think you may be right, devil. And I could heat it up in the microwave in less than a minute."

The devil pats you on the back. "Now you're thinking like a real saint. Go to it!"

I have these kinds of conversations all day long with the devil. Whenever something comes up that I know I should do, he pops up with three reasonable reasons why I shouldn't do it. It astonishes me sometimes. The worst part of it all, though, is the fact that I argue with him. Contrast that response with how Jesus answered Satan in the wilderness. For each temptation Satan slung His way, Jesus offered a simple verse of Scripture prefaced with three words: "It is written." Jesus didn't argue. He didn't offer His "humble opinion." He didn't even tell Satan to leave Him alone. He said, "It is written," and then shouted out a plain and simple Scripture tailored to the situation. Marvelous!

LEVELS OF TEMPTATION

On the face of it, Satan's first temptation of Jesus is simple. Jesus was obviously hungry, at the point of death. His body screamed for food. Nonetheless, the Father had made it clear: "You can eat only in My timing." That's not in the text, but Jesus, living in complete submission to His Father, must have been commanded to perform this fast. He certainly wasn't doing it for fun. He had been "led" to this point by the Spirit.

Luke says Jesus was tempted by the devil "for forty days." It appears that while both Matthew and Luke record the peak of the temptations, Satan had actually fought Jesus spiritually during the whole time. We don't know what those other temptations were, but certainly they only increased in severity as they went along.

Strangely enough, this particular temptation mimics the first temptation of Adam and Eve in the Garden. God forbade them to eat of a certain tree. With Jesus, the Father forbade eating at all until He gave the order.

More important, there appear to be several levels on which Satan is tempting Jesus. The most obvious was the sheer physical hunger Jesus experienced. Some suggest Satan was appealing to the "lust of the flesh." That may be true, but it's much deeper than that. Satan struck at the point of Jesus' most immediate and conscious need. Still, Satan wasn't just trying to get Jesus to eat. The temptation wasn't that He gorge Himself or satisfy a legitimate need. It was more a matter of will. This was the second level of temptation: Would Jesus obey God or someone else?

The issue here was obedience. God commanded that Jesus fast. To break the fast prematurely became an act of disobedience. It comes down to the simple biblical dictum: "submit to God." The Father desires our obedience. It's more important to Him than any amount of service, giving, or good deeds.

Without obedience everything else is meaningless. The Christian cannot say, "I love God," and then disobey His commands. Love involves submission, obedience, voluntary assent, and agreement with His Word through the right action.

When non-Christians offer a Christian teenager drugs, saying, "Go ahead, it'll feel good," they're voicing the words of Satan to Jesus, "Command that these stones become bread."

When the devil counsels a manager to hedge on his expense accounts, saying, "It's all right; everyone else does it. And anyway, you deserve it," the devil's using the age-old tactic he learned in Eden.

When a wife and husband quarrel, and a voice inside their heads interjects, "Give it to him [or her] with both barrels; he has no right to treat you like this!" it's no different from the devil's taunt to Jesus.

Any time we face a decision that suggests, "You don't have to obey God, He's being unreasonable. Do what you want," we're facing the devil's number-one tactic: will you obey God or me?

DEEPER COMMITMENT

Yet, obedience wasn't all that was at stake here. There's something still deeper. When Satan challenged Jesus to turn stones into bread, he wanted Jesus to suspect the Father's motives. In effect, he was saying, "What right does God have to do this to You? You shouldn't have to put up with this. It's not right. It's unfair. And You should be allowed to make Your own decision in this matter."

It comes down to trust. Will I trust the Father's judgment on this issue — even if I don't understand — or will I go my own way? Notice what God was asking of His Son: "I want You to fast for forty days. You'll be alone in the wilderness. I'm going to let Satan hurl all he's got at You. He'll tempt You to question My judgment. He'll suggest that I don't have Your best interests at heart. He'll scream that I'm being recklessly nasty for no good reason. But I want You to remember one thing: trust Me. I know what I'm doing. Just obey Me and it will all work out."

Think of the teenage girl in love with her boyfriend. He

wants her to have sexual relations with him. All these wonderfully fuzzy feelings pour over her in his presence. And she just can't understand why God says, "No, you must wait till you're married." It doesn't make sense to her. But that's the point of real obedience: when we choose to go God's way even though we may not understand why in all cases.

Think of a graduate student who cheats on an exam. He knows he should own up to his error. But he's afraid the prof will flunk him. What should he do? If he consults Scripture, God's commands will be plain. But going through with it will be difficult. "What if I do flunk? What if they expel me?" He must choose to trust God or go his own way, to his peril.

As Jesus and Satan faced off in the wilderness, clearly much more was at stake than simply turning stones into bread. Satan was challenging Jesus' whole concept of His Father: Can I trust Him completely?

THE PROCESS

Notice several elements of the temptation. First, Satan taunted and goaded Jesus. When he said, "If You are the Son of God," it was an "I dare You" tactic. Satan was saying more than "prove it!" He was appealing to something basic in our human nature—the desire not to be misunderstood, the longing that the truth be known.

One of my favorite movies is *Back to the Future*. In the film, the comment that continually places Marty McFly in the direst straits is the line, "What are you—chicken?" He always replies, "Nobody calls me chicken!" And he then proceeds to further entrap himself into a more tangled situation.

In a way, this is one of the devil's best tactics. When someone at the office insults you, what does the devil whisper? "Hey, you're a child of God, aren't you? Should you have to put up with this? So go ahead, let him have it—with both guns. You're Clint Eastwood, right?"

When you're caught in traffic, late for an appointment, and sensing that the deal is already lost, what does Satan murmur? "If I were you, I'd let God know in no uncertain terms what you think of His plan for today!"

Satan thrives on goading us. It's one of the best ways to get us to sin.

Notice also that turning stones into bread was something Jesus could do. Indeed, it was no problem for the Creator of the universe. In that respect, Satan only tempts us with things we can really fulfill and do. He'd never tell us to turn our set of dominoes into Godiva chocolates, but he might suggest we buy a box next time we're at the mall. He won't come at us with the idea of robbing a bank, but he could lead us to overload our credit cards till we break under the debt.

A big part of the problem of temptation is that we can so easily meet the desire. In most cases the devil tempts us with things that we can accomplish quickly and easily. The harsh criticism, the curse word, the quick but foolish purchase at the mall, the hour frittered away—all of them are the results of basic temptations. But they make up the fabric of what can become a failed Christian life.

Even more than this is the fact that Satan was appealing to a real and legitimate need on Jesus' part. He was hungry. He was at the point of starvation. He needed food, any food. He had nowhere to get it quickly—he was deep in the desert.

This is what often makes temptation so much harder to bear. So many of Satan's approaches concern legitimate, real, and natural concerns we all have. Whether it's the need for sleep, food, sex, recreation, money, shelter, or clothing, the devil can always put a sly spin on impropriety that makes it appear not as bad, or even beneficial.

JESUS' RESPONSE

Jesus responded to Satan in the classic way we're all taught from our early Christian days: He quoted Scripture. He said, "It is written, 'Man does not live on bread alone, but on every word that comes from the mouth of God.'" That command appears in Deuteronomy 8:3, as part of Moses' final exposition of the Law to the people of Israel before his death.

Moses spoke of Israel wandering in the wilderness for forty years. During that time, Moses says that God tested the people "in order to know what was in [their] heart, whether or not [they] would keep His commands." It's probable that as Jesus fasted in the wilderness He meditated on passages like this, particularly because they paralleled His own immediate experience. God tested Him for forty days in the wilderness.

Moses goes on to say to the Israelites that God "humbled you, causing you to hunger and then feeding you with manna . . . to teach you that man does not live on bread alone but on every word that comes from the mouth of God."

The story of the showering of manna is found in Exodus 16. The people had left Elim and penetrated the wilderness. They grew hungry, so they "grumbled" against Moses and Aaron. They accused them of bringing the nation into the wilderness to starve them. It was at that point that God sent the manna. But He sent it for a specific reason: "In this way I will test them and see whether they will follow My instructions" (v. 4). What were the instructions? To gather manna for five days, but on the sixth to gather a double portion because they were not to gather anything on the seventh.

Again, it was a test of obedience: Will you do it God's way or your way? Israel failed.

Undoubtedly, Jesus thought about Israel's failure as He stood alone and hungry in the wilderness on the far side of the Jordan River. Perhaps that was why He chose to answer Satan's temptation with this text. It was the right response for His own circumstances.

QUOTING GOD'S WORD

Why quote God's Word when tempted? There are several good reasons. First, it provides authority. Opinions in temptation lead only to argument. And when you argue with the devil, you inevitably lose. But the Word offers a heavenly fortress of authoritative power. When you quote it, you realize what God's will is. There can be no question, no altercation. "God said it, I believe it, that settles it!"

Second, quoting the word organizes your thinking. Satan's primary object is turmoil. When an army confuses its enemy, it can easily rout them. Loss of contact with "central control" spells defeat. Satan can twist us in deceit, befuddle us with reasonable reasons, and obliterate us with overpowering argumentation. But one line of Scripture settles everything. It clears the mind. It makes everything plain and simple.

Third, quoting the Word helps us withstand assault. One of the devil's best weapons is leading us to doubt God's Word. Isn't that what he did with Eve? Telling us, "God is wrong.

He made a mistake" is one strategy. Another is, "You're wrong; you're mistaken; God didn't say that." This is why knowing the Word letter-perfect so that you quote it precisely is so critical to success. If the devil challenges our quotation and we're unsure of the exact meaning or context, he'll annihilate us. But when we know and quote the Word with confidence, we can withstand any assault. The Word fortifies our faith.

Fourth, quoting the Word ends all argument. So long as we fling mere opinion into the fray, we'll get nothing but another opinion. But God's Word is final.

Finally, quoting the Word reinforces us in our convictions. The simple act of saying it out loud or reminding ourselves of its truth has spiritual power. God's Word is alive (Heb. 4:12) and God-breathed, according to 2 Timothy 3:16-17.

CAUTIONARY ADVICE

Still, when we use the Word, we can't simply haul off with, "John 3:16, Satan." Rather, we should quote Scripture:

With comprehension of its meaning and application. We can't reel off verses that have nothing to do with the situation. John 3:16 won't provide much punch when we face the temptation to lie to our boss. Romans 8:28 is a wonderful text, but it doesn't provide much insight when we're tempted to tell a questionable joke. It's important not only to know the meaning of the text, but also to log into our hearts plenty of such texts so we know where to look when we need them.

In context. Which of us hasn't recited a verse like John 10:10, "I came that they might have life and have it more abundantly," when we're down and troubled and need a helping hand? But often it seems that all that does is throw gasoline on the fire. Have you ever heard someone use the same verse to prove that Jesus wants us all to be healthy all the time, everywhere, at every minute? Taking a verse out of context not only amuses the devil, but it opens a way for him to assault us further with doubt when we find the verse doesn't work out in reality.

With conviction that it's correct. Quoting Scripture accomplishes nothing if we don't also believe it. One young man I interviewed repeatedly suffered anxiety attacks. He memorized Philippians 4:6-7, the passage that begins, "Be anxious for nothing." Yet, when anxiety struck, no amount of quoting the verse helped. Later, he realized he just didn't believe prayer could help him. His unbelief made it impossible for God to work in him.

With commitment to obey its directives. Ultimately, no amount of quoting the Bible will succeed unless we're also determined to obey what it says. A man struggling with lust might quote Matthew 5:28 over and over as he battles against his sin. (It says, "I tell you that anyone who looks at a woman lustfully has already committed adultery with her in his heart.") If he keeps "looking," then he'll lose the battle. He must obey not only by quoting it, but by living it out.

THE TRUTH OF THE ISSUE

Jesus' first temptation came down to an issue of obedience and trust. "Will I obey the Father's commandments? Can I trust Him even though I don't know why He commanded Me to do this?" When He quoted Deuteronomy 8:3, He pinned Satan to the wall. He was saying, "The issue here isn't food, devil. I'll get that in due time. The issue is My obedience to My Father, My trust that He has My best interests at heart. Food will get Me through the hour, but obeying Him will spring Me into eternity whole and joyous. I don't live — spiritually or emotionally — by consuming bread. I live by the words — the life, presence, and love — of God. Real life is sustained only by God. And I trust Him to meet My needs in His way."

Obedience.

Trust.

That's what was at stake at that moment in the wilderness. Christ obeyed because He trusted. It's the same with us. Sin that tempts us to go our way rather than God's is the crux of this issue. If we trust Him, we will obey Him. If we do not, we cannot. Victory starts with trust. A commitment to obedience leads us to make the right choice. Just as the song says, "Trust and obey, for there's no other way to be happy in Jesus than to trust and obey."

I CAN MATCH THAT!

CHAPTER 10

Winston Churchill mastered the snappy comeback, or repartee as it's called in polite society. Two of my favorite stories demonstrate his ability to turn a phrase. On one occasion officials at Whitehall — the English Pentagon — returned a memo that Churchill wrote on defense preparedness. They reprimanded him: "Do not end sentences with a preposition." Churchill immediately penned a response underneath: "This is pedantic nonsense up with which I will not put."[1]

On another occasion in 1959, Churchill spent too much time in the antechamber of the House of Commons imbibing alcoholic refreshment. As Sir Winston staggered to the House Chamber, a hefty Labourite opponent, Bessie Braddock, waddled toward the same door. In the collision that occurred Bessie fell flat on her ample behind. Getting up, she stormed, "Sir Winston, you are drunk. What's more, you are

[1]James C. Humes, *Podium Humor* (New York: Harper and Row, 1975), p. 280.

disgustingly drunk." Churchill looked Bessie up and down and then answered, "And you, Mrs. Braddock, are ugly. What's more, you are disgustingly ugly. Furthermore, tomorrow, I, Winston Churchill, shall be sober."[2]

Most of us can admire a quick-witted bit of humor even if it's not very complimentary. In some ways the second temptation Satan threw at Jesus in the wilderness, although not humorous, qualifies as a genuine satanic comeback. Jesus settled the first test with a deft recall of Deuteronomy 8:3. Satan thus chose to whisk Jesus off to the pinnacle of the temple where he tried again to fell the Master with his own quotation of Scripture—this time from Psalm 91.

The devil knows his Bible, at least enough to pick out a potent response. Perhaps he even anticipated what Jesus would say and shrewdly selected a few passages that might advance his cause. Shakespeare has Antonio say in *The Merchant of Venice,* "The devil can cite Scripture for his purpose."[3] Shakespeare may even have been referring to this very text.

THE SCENE

The scene is the pinnacle of the temple. "Pinnacle" means "wing," and it was most likely an edge of the roof on top of Herod's portico. It hung over the Kidron Valley, a drop of nearly 450 feet. Obviously, Satan had the power to transport Jesus to this site, which says much about the abilities the devil has. God limits him now. But there are and will be times when the Father lifts the restraints on Satan and his assembly and allows them to make full use of their spiritual, physical, and psychic capacities. Imagine what deceptions they will foist on mankind when—in the end times—God releases them to do their worst.

Satan places Him there and offers this crafty suggestion: "If You are the Son of God, throw Yourself down. For it is written, 'He will command His angels concerning You, and they will lift You up in their hands, so You will not strike Your foot against a stone.' "

Some theologians suggest that Satan had the idea that

[2]Humes, *Podium Humor,* pp. 1–2.

[3]John Bartlett, *Familiar Quotations* (New York: Little, Brown, and Co., 1955), p. 144.

Jesus, in leaping off the temple and plummeting to the ground, would be seen by the crowd below. As the angels caught Him, the observers would respond with instant recognition of His power and messiahship. Thus, Jesus would accomplish a part of His purpose — to be acclaimed as the Messiah — in one daunting act.

There are problems with that idea. First, if Jesus did take Satan's bait, it would do nothing to help Satan's cause. How would such recognition be a gain for the devil? Second, Jesus knew the fickleness of the people. His miracles did little to permanently convince anyone of His deity. In fact, Jesus said in Luke 16:31 that those who rejected Moses and the prophets would not believe even if someone came to them from the dead. Third, there's no mention of a crowd. If impressing them was Satan's purpose, then why didn't he mention it?

WHAT WAS AT STAKE?

What I believe was going on here follows from the first temptation. Jesus concluded Satan's initial test with a statement of complete trust in His Father. He would obey because He trusted Him. As a result, Satan points Jesus to a test that will "prove" God's trustworthiness. He is saying, "All right, You trust Your Father. Then why not find out right now how reliable He is? Jump off the temple. He promises in Psalm 91 to protect You. Why not make sure of His dependability now, before You go on any further, get into trouble, and find out He won't help You?"

Years ago, a movie about the life of Rosemary Clooney, the singer, portrayed her descent into depression, alcoholism, and family estrangement. One night in a last-ditch effort to resurrect her life, she drove down the road at night through the rain on the *wrong side* of the highway. As she drove, she screamed at God, "If You love me, You won't let me die!"

Satan proposed the same plot. "If He loves You, Jesus, He won't let You die. So find out right now! Test Him! Prove it once and for all."

LIFE'S GREATEST ISSUE

The issue of whether or not we can trust God ranks as life's most difficult problem. Every command in Scripture hinges on this point. Every promise, every truth about the Father, Son, and Spirit, is ultimately an issue of trust. Can we proceed in faith, believing that God will indeed protect, guide, fortify, advise, comfort, and encourage us, or must we demand to live by sight and force Him to prove His love?

Satan tests us on this issue in a multitude of ways. For instance . . .

A woman dying of cancer is tempted to believe God has deserted her because she is not healthy.

A man struggling with alcohol addiction tells God he'll only believe Him if He'll take away the thirst overnight.

A Christian man decides to marry a non-Christian woman. Although he knows that Scripture forbids such a union, he challenges God to do "some special miracle" to prove to him he shouldn't go through with it.

A high school senior who recently stopped using cocaine is tempted to go to a party where he knows drugs will abound. He prays that God will help him resist the temptation.

Jay Carty offers an interesting perspective in his book, *Counterattack*. He refers to the problem of "eclairs in your refrigerator." Carty pictures a scene in which a woman on a diet succumbs to temptation and buys two chocolate eclairs on her way home from work. When she finally gets home, though, guilt overtakes her and she places the eclairs in the fridge, then rushes into the living room to pray, "Lord, help me not eat those eclairs!"

Carty points out the contradiction. She prayed for power, but she kept the eclairs safe in the icebox. Why? In case she wanted them later when she didn't feel so guilty about it! In other words, she prayed for one thing but acted in contradiction to her prayers. Carty's counsel is to get rid of the eclairs — not by consuming them, but by depositing them in the local dumpster.[4]

Temptation increases or decreases according to the availability of the tempting object or idea. If what you want is only three steps away, it's much harder to resist than when you have to drive across country to get it.

Nonetheless, let's take that illustration and examine it an-

---

[4] Jay Carty, *Counterattack* (Portland, Ore.: Multnomah Press, 1988), pp. 29–30.

other way. Recall the lady on a diet who decides to "test" herself with eclairs. She hangs around the eclair store just to see how well she can resist. She walks by the eclair shop at the mall and even gives them a mouth-watering sniff, while at the same time telling herself she's just testing to see how God will empower her. After all, if God really loves her, He'll give her the strength to resist anything.

Mahatma Gandhi, the Indian politician and spiritual guru, used to test his ability to fend off lust by sleeping with naked and beautiful girls. He did nothing with them sexually. But he enjoyed testing his concentration so that even in the presence of such a beauty he would feel no arousal.

While that might have been good for Gandhi, it's utter foolishness for most of us. We dare not test the Lord or even test ourselves with temptations. The first rule is to get out of the tempting situation, not to confront it head-on.

SATAN'S USE OF SCRIPTURE

Notice how Satan used Scripture in this passage. He took his text from Psalm 91, a psalm about God's great and wondrous protection in evil times. Arrows may fly around you, a thousand soldiers might be cut down to your right and left. But you will walk through the battle unharmed—if you make God your dwelling place.

The psalm speaks explicitly about the need to "walk" with God. As we make God our dwelling place, as we live in His presence and trust Him to uphold us, we will find He always comes to our aid when we are in a desperate situation. God says, "Because he loves Me, I will rescue him; I will protect him, for he acknowledges My name" (Ps. 91:14).

But the devil offers his own spin on this text. In Matthew's account of the Temptation, he leaves out several words of the psalm (though Luke's passage includes part of what he left out). Satan says, "He will command His angels concerning You," and leaves off the next phrase, "to guard You in all Your ways." What is the significance of this omission? Some suggest that Satan left this part off because it means God will guard you "as you walk in righteousness"—"your ways." But the word "way" simply means road or path. The psalmist is saying that God will guard you wherever you go. In effect, that would even seem to support Satan's contention. "Go ahead, jump! God will guard you wherever you go."

What I believe happened here provides a key insight about the devil. He failed to quote that line not because it failed to support his purpose, but more likely because he simply didn't think it was necessary. It was redundant, and he wanted to get out the line as quickly as possible. Remember, Satan not only twists the truth, but he scorns it as well. He approaches it rather lazily and will only do what he thinks is necessary to fry his catch. He doesn't waste words. He regards the truth with contempt and therefore treats it haphazardly. Even with the Son of God, he was more concerned to hurry Him into the trap—knowing that hasty decisions favor his side—than to get Jesus to think about something he might have omitted.

The real problem with Satan's quotation is that it's ripped out of its context. Psalm 91 promises protection to the person who obeys, loves, and trusts God in the midst of difficult situations. If a storm comes up, the psalmist is saying, "trust God—He'll protect you. If you're fighting on the front lines, don't worry—God will protect you." It doesn't mean He will always see you through physical danger, only that we'll arrive in heaven safe and intact. Like Paul said in 2 Timothy 4:18: "The Lord will rescue me from every evil attack and will bring me safely to His heavenly kingdom."

Evangelist Joe Boyd used to tell a story about a man he knew who lost his index finger. Joe asked what happened and the man replied, "A snake bit me when the stick broke." The man had kept a six-foot rattlesnake as a pet. Normally caged, one day he took it out to taunt his wife. When she fled in terror, he pinned the snake's head to the floor with a forked stick. The snake writhed angrily. The man leaned on the stick heavily to hold it in position. Suddenly the stick cracked, the snake reared back and struck, injecting its venom into the man's finger. A doctor saved his life, but the finger was amputated.

Satan's second temptation of Jesus was much like the story of that rattlesnake. Satan taunted Jesus to prove that God would keep Him from being bitten. Jesus' reply demonstrates the foolishness of such a challenge.

SCRIPTURE TWISTING

What are some of the texts that Satan twists for his own purposes? Consider some of the following:

Philippians 4:13: "I can do everything through Him who gives me strength." Some interpret this to mean we can accomplish anything in life that we set our minds to. But other verses provide the balance: God will only enable us to do what it is His will to do (see 1 John 5:14-15). The context of this verse speaks about being content in adverse circumstances. Paul means he can remain contented and happy through Christ even when times are tough.

Philippians 4:19: "My God will meet all your needs according to His glorious riches in Christ Jesus." Some take this to mean we will all prosper materially in this world. We'll get rich, if we'll only trust. That's Satan's setup for a big letdown. When we don't prosper the way we believe we should, we begin to doubt God and His Word. This verse actually refers to God's provision for "need"—basic and general needs, not overflowing riches—and only in the context of our giving sacrificially to help others.

Matthew 6:33: "Seek first His kingdom and His righteousness, and all these things will be given to you as well." Again, Satan contorts this to mean we will prosper materially, emotionally, and physically. But the context refers only to basic needs: food and clothing.

Jeremiah 29:11: "For I know the plans I have for you . . . plans to prosper you and not to harm you, plans to give you hope and a future." Again the promise of prosperity and our immunity from harm. Christians who claim this verse believe nothing bad can happen to them. But Christians do lose jobs, suffer bankruptcy, experience loss of loved ones, and contract terrible diseases. Jeremiah spoke this promise specifically to the Jews exiled in Babylon to get them to return to faith in God. It's simply not a promise of absolute prosperity and an assurance of protection from everything in this world.

Acts 1:8 tells us that we shall be "witnesses" of Christ. Satan twists this verse by placing a huge load of guilt on us when we don't witness. He can turn us into compulsive "tellers of the Gospel" who forget all the other biblical values of consideration, tact, kindness, love, and example. At one time

I felt an evening spent with a non-Christian wasn't profitable unless I "shared the Gospel." But what I discovered was that there is a time to listen and keep quiet as well as a time for sharing. I believe Satan enjoys "compulsive witnessing" as much as failure to witness at all. Both fail to communicate the real message of love, forgiveness, and understanding.

1 Peter 3:7: "Husbands, in the same way be considerate as you live with your wives, and treat them with respect." Sometimes the devil uses a wife to put down and degrade a husband because she feels he's not being "considerate" and "respectful." She uses the text as a club to beat him over the head with guilt. He makes faulty decisions based not on what is best for the family, but what will gain his wife's approval.

1 Peter 3:1: "Wives, in the same way be submissive to your husbands." By the same token, Satan distorts the whole idea of submission into the abject picture of wife as doormat, one who just takes everything and never makes a peep. Husbands batter their wives into "submission" as well with angry quotes of this verse. Scripture never calls for a submission that has no rights, never speaks up, never offers an opinion, never asks that her own needs be met. There's a balance here, and it can only be found through studying the context of Scripture.

Colossians 3:21: "Fathers, provoke not your children to anger, lest they be discouraged." Satan rips this one right out of context and advises fathers not to discipline their kids. He also twists the previous verse (v. 20) that calls for children to obey their parents to mean that they never have a say in anything and can't make honest requests of their parents, or that they must obey unconscionable, even immoral things. Neither condition is true.

1 John 1:9, a well-known memory verse about confessing our sins. The devil creates plenty of misery for saints who wonder if they've confessed everything or confessed it enough or if they've left anything out. The Scripture assures us that if we confess what we're aware of as sin, God will cleanse us from anything we're not aware of.

1 Peter 4:8: "Love covers over a multitude of sins." Again, the devil scrambles this up so that we think it means we should put up with every offense, never challenging a sinner's behavior. The "judge not lest you be judged" idea is similar. Some people believe no Christian should ever "judge" another who is sinning. They believe he should pray that God would wake the sinner up to his errors. The truth is that we are called "to speak the truth in love" (Eph. 4:14-16), confront erring brethren (Matt. 18:15-17), and "restore" sinners to a state of spiritual health (Gal. 6:1). Love does indeed "cover" many of the foibles, idiosyncracies, and sinful words and deeds that many of us do unconsciously. But there's also a time to take a saint to task if the sin has become a genuine spiritual problem.

1 Thessalonians 5:16: "Pray continually." Some Christians can never be happy about their prayer life, believing that they always fall short of this command. But the meaning is that we're to pray as often as we think of it or need it. It doesn't say we should carry on a running monologue toward heaven every minute of the day.

SATAN'S SCRIPTURAL TACTICS

Satan typically does three things with Scripture. He takes it out of context, as we've seen above. He twists it out of proportion to its original intent (like the snake-handling cults that believe that the reference to "picking up snakes" in Mark 16:18 is a command to handle deadly serpents in faith). And he also emphasizes some Scripture out of balance to other Scriptures.

Context speaks of the immediate circumstance of the actual passage. Proportion refers to the relation of the verse to other biblical verses. Balance considers the light of the whole Bible on a truth. This knowledge of balance was precisely why Jesus chose to respond to Satan's words with the statement, "It is written, 'Do not put the Lord your God to the test.' "

It's a point of balance. "Yes, it's true God will protect Me," Jesus answers, "but there's a balancing truth about His protection. I'm not to put Myself in harmful situations just to make Him protect Me. That's not what the Father offers to do at all."

PUTTING GOD TO THE TEST

How do we put God to the test? Any dangerous situation that we might encourage to see what He will do is putting Him to the test. Jesus undoubtedly thought of Deuteronomy 6:16, which says, "Do not test the Lord your God as you did at Massah." The original verse is part of a series of brief commands about how we're to treat God. Only a few verses earlier is the most famous passage in all the Old Testament, at least to Jews. It's called the Shema. "Hear, O Israel: the Lord our God, the Lord is One. Love the Lord your God with all your heart and with all your soul and with all your strength." Jews who observe religious tradition typically repeat this passage when they come into a house, into the temple, and before prayer.

The point of Jesus' statement, though, was that we should not test God the same way Israel tested Him at Massah.

In Exodus 17:1-7 we read how the people of Israel cried out for water. It was certainly a legitimate request. But their problem was the way they approached it. They accused God of bringing them out of Egypt to kill them. They complained and grumbled. They attacked God's character. Finally, they said, "Is the Lord among us or not?" In other words, they were saying, "Prove You love us, prove You care, prove You can do as You say—and give us water. NOW!" They didn't come to God humbly and present a simple request with the expectation that He would gladly comply. No, they hauled back their fists and screamed in His face, "We won't believe You can do anything until You give us something to drink." It was a virtual insult.

In the same way, leaping off the pinnacle of the temple to find out if God would catch Him would be equally insulting. Yet, it's an old tactic of the devil's. The child says to the mother, "If you love me, you'll buy me that toy." The boy says to his girlfriend, "If you really care about me, you'd give me what I want." The wife says to her husband, "If you honestly love me, you'd give in to my wishes." And on and on. Christians set up such tests not only when they put themselves in danger to see if God will protect them, but also when they ask for "signs," put out fleeces (as Gideon did in Jud. 6:36-40), or demand that He answer certain prayers or "we won't believe." Either we trust Him or we don't. If we do trust Him, we won't demand that He perform miracles in order to prove His worth.

BUILDING FAITH

Ultimately, what Satan was suggesting was, "The way to build faith is to challenge God to come through on His Word," or even more bluntly, "Put yourself in a position where He has to come through or else!"

We see this kind of "faith-building" all over our world. Christians "claim" a so-called promise of God in the name of faith and commitment. They "demand" health, a prosperous business, a healing, or a change in behavior on the basis of the "greatness and glory of God." It's all little more than an insult. We're "daring" Him to act on our behalf because we believe so intensely.

This isn't real faith. True faith does not live by sight, but on "every word that proceeds out of the mouth of God." The person of faith acts on God's Word in a responsible, balanced, honest, and forthright manner. He does not "put God in a box" or "in a corner." He never makes "demands" on God, or "claims" preposterous acts in the name of His Word. Rather, as Micah said, he acts justly, loves mercy, and walks humbly with his God (Micah 6:8). God supports those "whose heart is completely His" (2 Chron. 16:9). God is not a toy we wind up and set spinning to do as we please. He's Master, Lord, Sovereign, and Friend. He longs for our trust on the basis of who He is and what He is, not what He does.

To be sure, if we obey His Word, He will bless us. If we follow His commands, He will fill our lives with every good thing. But His acts in our lives should not change our level of trust. When the first Christians faced the lions, they didn't say, "I'll only trust You if You shut their mouths like you did for Daniel." No, they sang even as the maws of the lions tore their throats. They trusted because of God's Word, not because they witnessed miracles. Even the disciples didn't believe on the basis of Jesus' multitude of miracles. They believed only when the Holy Spirit came upon them.

GET THE SCOPE OF SCRIPTURE IN YOUR MIND

In the end, this test gets at the whole issue of how we express our trust in God. Do we pray for some incredible answer, then react with doubt in His goodness or existence because He didn't come through as we wanted? Do we believe His Word and act on it, or do we cry out for Him to give us some mystical "power" before we'll try to obey? Do we work to understand the full scope of Scripture, or have we simply memorized a few texts and decided that is enough?

In the first temptation Jesus demonstrates the need to know and obey basic truths of the Bible. He shows how powerful a simple word from God can be in an extreme situation of abject hunger.

In the second temptation, Jesus illuminates the need to know the breadth and balance of Scripture. It's not enough simply to know a text. We must grow to the place where we can weave the many threads of the Bible into a tapestry for circumspect living. Like Paul told Titus, an elder must be able to "encourage others by sound doctrine and refute those who oppose it" (Titus 1:9). Refuting the devil's erroneous arguments requires a careful and sensitive eye. We must not only be able to spot error, but also to dissect truth mixed with error. That calls for a daily diet of Scripture reading and memorization so that our minds become imbued with the Bible's words.

Arturo Toscanini, the great symphony conductor, gained a reputation as an astute and sensitive interpreter of music. He often conducted whole symphonies from memory, without so much as a single page of a score in front of him. On one occasion during a rehearsal, a second violinist grazed a string next to the correct one by accident. Few musicians present noticed it. But Toscanini stopped the proceedings, leveled his baton at the errant violinist, and quipped sharply, "One string will be quite enough, if you please."

Ultimately, it's that kind of sensitivity that God seeks to bring us to in our encounters with temptation and sin. He longs that we become so immersed in truth that the slightest deviation fires off a spiritual cannon shot in our minds. He wants us to see sin so clearly that we spot it as deftly and easily as Toscanini pinpointed a missed note in a fifty-piece violin section. Without such clarity of mind and precision of heart, we are little more than meat scraps awaiting the gnash of a roaring lion.

THE HEART
OF THE ISSUE

CHAPTER 11

Years ago my family visited the Gettysburg battlefield in
Pennsylvania. As we toured the area, my father ex-
pounded on the great generals and leaders during those
dark days. We gazed on statues and memorials to the Southern generals Longstreet, Pickett, and Lee. We learned of how
Lincoln prior to the battle had fired General Hooker as commander of the Northern troops and appointed George Meade
in his place, and how during the three-day battle Meade bril-
liantly stopped Robert E. Lee's march north. We examined
the deadly minié balls that the soldiers fired and dreamed of
finding one in a clump of dirt while scouring the battlefield
itself.

But the place and moment that lives most vividly in my
memory was my first sight of the huge mural of the "Bloody
Angle." Pickett's charge, in which over 15,000 Southern
troops assaulted 10,000 Northerners on Cemetery Ridge, left
me in awe. At one point the fighting swirled around a stone
wall called the "Bloody Angle." It was the high-water mark of

Lee's invasion of the North. Southern troops never got any farther. It was in a sense the South's final effort to win the Civil War.

In any battle there comes a moment when the enemy throws everything he's got at his adversary, seeking to overwhelm him with his might and audacity. Some fights like that have a kind of glory attached to them. We remember the great battles of history: Thermopylae; Waterloo; Verdun; El Alamein; the Battle of the Bulge; Midway. Each had its decisive point, a moment when all seemed to be lost or won.

Satan also had such a moment. I suspect that for Jesus the third temptation was little more than an irritating nip at His heels. But when Satan placed Jesus on that "very high mountain" and showed Him "all the kingdoms of the world in an instant," as Luke says, he used his best guile and deception in a remarkable final effort. He offered Jesus "all the kingdoms of the world and their splendor." He says in Luke's passage that it "had been given to him" and he could give it to whomever he wanted. All he wanted in return was a brief act of worship.

Could Jesus fake it?

Could He have bowed the knee with His fingers crossed?

Was it even a tempting proposition to Him?

SATAN'S THOUGHTS

Looking at the temptation as it's written in Matthew and Luke, it's difficult to picture Jesus even considering this bauble. Yet for a moment, consider what a bauble it was: all the kingdoms of the world. At that time there was Rome. That might have been enough to take anyone's breath away. But certainly Satan had the power to project a vision of India and China as well, perhaps even the peoples of Africa, Australia, and the Americas. On that high mountain, Satan displayed before Jesus a golden-tinged splendor: the armies, the riches, the magnificent buildings, the people. All of it. One stunning moment. One gleaming vision of greatness, wealth, pleasure.

If I had been Jesus, I can imagine what He could have thought—if Satan's deception was working. First of all, He might have thought the cross would no longer be necessary. He'd get the world back without any pain.

Of course, that assumption is incorrect. Jesus didn't come to get back buildings, horses, gold, and armies. He came for the hearts of people, which could only be bought with His blood.

Second, He might have considered how nice it would be to have that kind of power. After all, He grew up in poverty. He would live a life of pain, ending with an ignominious and terrifying death. All that might be avoided, and there would be plenty of fun to boot.

But again, I can't see that thought even grazing Jesus' mind. He was God incarnate. He owned it all to begin with. He ruled with His Father from heaven. He knew what it was like to possess unlimited power, not just worldly power. This was little more than a trinket to Him.

So what was the temptation?

SOME QUALIFICATIONS

Let's qualify it.

First, there's this display of things like

power
plenitude
pleasure
prestige
popularity
peace

Most of us long for all these things. As a human being, Jesus must have been aware of these realities, what they were, what they meant for Him and others.

Second, there's a promise. "Do this; you'll get that." It's Satan's old and favored tactic. He did it with Eve. He does it with all of us. "Go my way and you'll get all these wonderful things at practically no cost."

In a way, Satan is correct. Sin does offer us pleasure, power, and whatnot for a small "up front" price in most cases (it will cost plenty in the long run, but he never brings that part up). All of us experience the temptation to get the things we want in the wrong ways. God says real joy comes only through obedience to His Word. Satan offers "sinful joy" (a counterfeit with a high degree of *immediate* pleasure) at the "small" price of disobedience to God's principles. It's usually far easier to disobey than it is to obey.

Third, this is what Satan really wants from Jesus and from all of us: worship. Here is his real objective. Turning stones into bread was a warm-up. The scene atop the pinnacle was of secondary importance to Satan. But in this temptation Satan is offering us the whole pot. All we have to do is go along with the game and we'll win it.

Fourth, beyond this temptation Satan has nothing more to offer. This is his best shot. He's putting his money where his mouth is. Or so he would like us to think.

DID JESUS HAVE DIFFICULTY WITH THIS TEMPTATION?

Yet, I still find it difficult to believe Jesus felt even His knees get slightly weak in the face of this offer. Was He really tempted? Did He feel any longing to cry, "Yes, I'll take it"? Was He even interested?

To some degree, we're all so familiar with this historic scene that it loses its luster. It covers barely two verses of Scripture—rather short ones at that—and we can easily slide over it without feeling moved.

But think about yourself for a moment. How do you feel when you see a glittering Mercedes glide by on its cushion suspension? Are you attracted?

What about a beautiful woman or a handsome man? Does Paul Newman, Tom Cruise, or Clint Eastwood flip your switch? How about Candice Bergen or Michelle Pfeiffer? Do you ever sense a covetous lust boiling up inside you?

What about that custom home you dream about? Does that get the juices flowing?

How about winning the Publisher's Weekly Sweepstakes? Or the lottery jackpot? Are they things you momentarily dream about?

Now imagine that this thing, person, or experience is dropped right on your front doorstep. It's there for the taking. You can have it—forever. It's yours.

Would you consider it? Would you be interested?

Of course, if you're as suspicious as I am of advertising scams, your first question would be, "What's the scheme? What's the gimmick? What's the price?"

"Oh, not much," the salesman replies. "For the Mercedes all you need do is invest in my retirement program."

"And what's that—forty grand a year?"

"No, actually, it's just a matter of agreeing to reside permanently in my little retirement village. Here, I'll show you the pictures."

What thoughts go through your head? "Retirement—that's a hundred years away. Besides, I can probably get out of it. Or the guy will die in the meantime. Or I'll move. Whatever, that's nothing." You say, "I'll take it."

So you sign your life away.

Now of course, it doesn't happen quite like that. It involves more of a gradual adherence to a worldly lifestyle and principles than actually making a "pact with the devil." But this is the catch: once you've sold out, there's no going back. Once you get into the devil's game, you cannot easily back out.

What I mean by that is this. At the moment that Jesus was offered all the kingdoms of the world and their glory (and we by the same token are given the choice of following Satan's path of materialism, hedonism, and selfishness or God's way), He was faced with a simple choice. He had to choose. But after the choice is made everything changes.

It's like losing your virginity. There's no going back. You can lie about it. You can pretend. But the decision was made, and the act completed.

In the same way, Jesus was confronted with the final decision: Will You choose God or Satan as Your Lord? I believe that every person who lives faces that decision. Once it's made, it's irrevocable. Jesus couldn't fake His worship. He couldn't choose Satan and then repent a few minutes later. This choice was presented to Him as the ultimate and final decision of His life. Yes, Satan would come back and haunt Him later. He would try to spoil His plans. He would attempt to lead Him astray in other ways.

But this third temptation delineates the dividing line of one's destiny.

A PERSONAL EXAMPLE

Let me give you an illustration. In January 1972 I was confronted for the first time in my life with the Gospel of Christ.

I read Hal Lindsey's book, *The Late Great Planet Earth,* and his words scared me into investigating the Bible and the person of Jesus. For nine months I read my Bible regularly and prayed. But God was not real. I used marijuana regularly. I got drunk. I practiced numerous forms of debauchery. In the back of my mind, I thought about Christ, but I had no idea of a relationship or a "walk" with Him.

Then that summer I conversed with a friend in which we discussed a number of philosophical issues: the meaning of life; where we were going as people; career decisions; and finally, the person of Jesus. At one point in our talk, I asked him, "Do you believe in Jesus Christ or God?" He told me he didn't know. Then he turned the question on me: "What about you?"

It was the first time in my life anyone asked me point-blank if I believed in Jesus. I knew if I told him yes, he might laugh at me. But I had been reading the Bible and praying. In my mind somehow I realized—without making any connection to eternal destiny, salvation, or anything else—that my answer counted. I couldn't simply blow it off. After a minute or so of thought, I answered with these words: "I don't know why, but I believe that Jesus Christ is the Son of God."

My friend snickered, but we moved on to other subjects. I forgot about the conversation.

The next morning, though, something inside me had changed. I wasn't sure what it was, but I felt almost light, free, at peace. Gradually, other things happened. I sensed a Presence I'd never known before. I felt as though I understood something deep in my bones about the meaning of life. I picked up a Bible and understood its words. They spoke directly to me. I sensed that God was communicating with me.

It was a marvelous experience. I was "born again." I was transformed. I gave up drugs and drinking. I reversed my thinking on things like the theory of evolution, premarital sex, Jesus as only a "good man," the Bible as "just another book," and numerous other issues. My whole life changed.

Now the question is: What if I had told my friend that night that I didn't believe in Jesus? What might have happened?

I sincerely believe that I would probably have lived the rest of my life like most other people. I would have a career, get married, ponder questions, struggle, debate, wonder about things. Perhaps God would have given me another chance, another point of decision. But I don't think so. I believe everyone of us is given a complete opportunity, like Jesus had in the wilderness with Satan. There may be a multitude of events leading up to our conversion. It could be years. We might hear the Gospel a hundred, a thousand times before we reach that moment.

But for all of us there is a time when God and Satan stand before us, and we must decide whose way we will go.

That was what Jesus faced at that moment in the wilderness. That was what I faced that August night in 1972. That is what all of us will face someday, if we have not already. The decision we make then is, I believe, irrevocable.

By that I don't mean that God is not sovereign in salvation, or that anyone can subvert His elective plan. Nor do I mean that we all have only one opportunity to believe. For each of us, life may present a multitude of opportunities to hear and believe the Gospel. Nor am I saying that if a person rejects Christ at one point in his life he cannot accept Him later. It's just that none of these lesser moments were the true moment of decision. Until that moment, each of us is just a person bumbling through life. We ask questions. We struggle. We fight within ourselves. We make decisions, then reverse them two minutes later. But when we face the final confrontation, our destiny is sealed: from that moment on we are either a child of God, or a pawn of Satan. There's no going back.

This is why I believe Jesus didn't try to turn back Judas Iscariot. When he went to the priests to betray Jesus, Judas had made his decision. There was no going back.

It's also why Romans 1 repeats the expression, "God gave them over," as we see people descend further and further into the pit. What preceded that descent? Romans 1:21 tells us: "For although they knew God, they neither glorified Him as God nor gave thanks to Him, but their thinking became futile, and their foolish hearts were darkened." Once they rejected God, they slipped irrevocably into a darker and deeper pit which they could never leave.

Does this mean a person can't make a "final" decision to reject Him at one point and then change his decision later? Of course not. But that "final" decision was not yet like the one that Jesus faced in the wilderness.

For all of us there is one ultimate decision. There's only one that counts, and that one places us in one camp or the other. It could occur on the last day of our lives. It might happen when we're three years old. For all of us it's different. But one thing is sure: it's the moment when we cross the line of destiny.

That moment was the last test Jesus faced in the wilderness. It had little to do with kingdoms, glory, or even circumventing the cross. It was for Him—and us—the ultimate test: will we love, honor, and worship God, or will we go another way?

For that reason, it was a struggle even for Jesus. He knew well what God the Father would require of Him. He understood where it was all going. He recognized the Father didn't promise peaches, cream, and weekends at the beach. The Father required complete obedience to the point of death. Could He take that? Would He accept that? Or would He find an easier way?

OBEDIENCE IN EVERYDAY LIFE

Of course, this same temptation presents itself in much more common ways. Satan doesn't change his tactics much, whether he's serving up sex, drugs, alcohol, money, or comfort. He uses the same tactics on all levels.

Thus, we can see that Jesus' temptation is also an illustration of something Satan does with all of us, even after we are born again and committed to God's kingdom and Person.

What is the process? I see several steps.

1. A promising possibility. Satan offers us something. He promises an experience, a pleasure, a reward in return for disobedience to God's principles.

2. The cultivation of a hunger for this possibility. The second step is that having heard what's possible, we begin nurturing and stoking the inner hunger for the illicit thing.

3. A convincing rationalization of Scripture. After that, we begin to twist and rationalize the truth on the issue.

We convince ourselves that somehow we won't truly be doing wrong.

4. A compromise of Scripture. At this point, we've decided not to listen to what the Word of God says. We go our own way, or in this case, Satan's.

5. Cautious experimentation. We get involved with sin in an experimental way. We "try it out" just to see what it's like. If we find it's not as bad as we were taught, we continue in our slide into the pit.

6. A continual giving in. Now we're committing the sin regularly. We enjoy it. We prefer it to God's dictums and promises.

7. The complete sellout. We reach the final stage where we no longer care what God says and we do as we please.

At any point along this line, there are always two possible other realities. One is

◊ **Confession of sin.** You can choose to halt the progress of your entrenchment in sin, confess it, be cleansed, and come back into fellowship. Or . . .

◊ **Confirmed rebellion.** You become more and more entrenched in your sin and unable to free yourself from it.

This is what happens with Satan's tactic of "bait and hitch." He baits us with the promise, and we get hitched to his program. It happens in nearly every kind of temptation we face. Sin promises instant gratification, pleasure, wealth, or power. We take the hook and find ourselves soon enmeshed in a net of sin that seems difficult to get out of.

CHRIST'S RESPONSE TO THE DEVIL

What was Jesus' response to Satan? He quoted Deuteronomy 6:13. The original passage says, "Fear the Lord your God, serve Him only and take your oaths in His name." It's found in the same paragraph as Jesus' response to the second temptation, which is only three verses further on. What was the context?

Moses referred in particular to the problem of the people arriving in Israel, prospering, being filled with every good thing, and then forgetting God. That problem plagued the Israelites from the beginning. How easy it is to forget God once you're doing well. It's like what Jesus said about rich people: "It's easier for a camel to go through the eye of a needle than for a rich man to enter the kingdom of God" (Matt. 19:24).

Perhaps what was on Jesus' mind at the moment of Satan's temptation was: "I see all this grandeur and glitter, but how can I forget My Father who has proved His goodness to Me over and over? How can I discard Him, especially in view of His love, care, and constant compassion to Me?"

He couldn't.

But that's also precisely what keeps us from going Satan's way. Even when things are hard, temptations are strong, and we wish to take the easy way out, we won't because we cannot hurt the One who has so loved us. We know that He alone is worthy of our love, our respect, and our service.

Notice what Jesus did. He responded *quickly*. There's no argumentation here, no inner fumbling. He immediately brought out the Word. The sooner we can do that in a temptation situation, the more likely we'll see a victory.

Second, He *quoted* Scripture again. Simple, but effective.

Third, His quotation *quelled* all argument. There was nothing left for the devil to do. So . . .

Fourth, the devil *quit*. Satan knew when he was beat.

How do we get to the point where we can defeat the devil this easily? It's simple:

1. Read Scripture and know what it says (1 Tim. 4:13).
2. Memorize as many verses as you can, and then keep on learning more (Ps. 119:11; Col. 3:16).
3. Study the passages for further insight (2 Tim. 2:15).
4. Meditate on them constantly (Josh. 1:8; Deut. 6:4-9; Prov. 6:20-23).
5. Practice God's Word in the context of life (Heb. 5:13-14).
6. Use the Word to solve problems (2 Tim. 3:16-17).
7. Pray for illumination of God's will for your life (1 John 5:14-15).
8. Share what you're learning (Eph. 5:18-20).

It's not real complicated. Jesus didn't use some incredible secret weapon to defeat the devil. He knew the Word. He used it. And the devil ran.

The same thing can happen with us.

RELIEF

What happened after the devil left Jesus? The text says, "Then the devil left Him, and angels came and attended Him." This was God's relief squad. They ministered to Jesus, probably fed Him, and helped Him relax after this harrowing experience. How does God spell relief?

R = Refreshment. The angels refreshed, rejuvenated, strengthened, and empowered Him (Matt. 4:11). Though we may not recognize it, angels undoubtedly minister to us in the same way.

E = Establishment. Peter says in 1 Peter 5:10 that after we have suffered, the God of all grace will Himself "restore you and make you strong, firm, and steadfast." *Restoration* speaks of a return to a former condition. It literally means to "mend." *Strength* obviously means spiritual strength, making someone strong so that he does not give in. *Firmness* speaks of an ability to persevere and not lose ground. It means to fix something firmly so that it cannot be moved. *Steadfastness* implies that a foundation is laid underneath us. It means placing beneath ourself a firm cement floor that will not be moved in times of trouble. Certainly God promises through such temptations to make us stronger, more resilient, better able to handle the circumstances of life.

L = Life. James says that once we have been approved through a trial, we'll "receive the crown of life that God has promised to those who love Him" (James 1:12). This intimates not only a future crown in His kingdom, but a present condition of joy in life that we can never experience without having gone through and defeated temptation. Whenever I've struggled with temptation and gained a victory, I find that a surge of joy, peace, and love fills me that can only qualify as life — God's life, the only kind that lets us really "live it up!"

I = Insight. Victory over temptation brings with it an uncanny result: the godly discernment of good and evil. We gain insight. Had Adam and Eve not succumbed in the Garden, they would have achieved the same result and gained such knowledge without sinning. But when we defeat temptation, we grow, we learn, we become better able to help others, and God grants us the experience to "distinguish good and evil" (Heb. 5:14).

E = Endurance. There is no more important quality to the Lord than endurance. James speaks of the enduring person as perfect and mature (James 1:2-4). Paul considered endurance the means to great spiritual growth, and he thanked God for the trials that led to it (see Rom. 5:1-5). Only the enduring person is the true "man of God" or "person of principle." It does no good to spout Christian ideas and not live them out by holding to them in the fray of battle.

F = Freedom. Ultimately, the final result of victory is freedom. Jesus said that when we "hold to His teaching" we prove our discipleship. And "then [we] will know the truth and the truth will set [us] free" (John 8:31-32). Paul assured us that God called us to "freedom" (see Gal. 5:1, 13). That freedom not only breaks the shackles of enslaving sin habits, but it also allows us to experience the fullness of His blessing.

The relief God provides us, in and after temptation, is like the thrill of rock-climbing. Have you ever scaled a cliff? When I tried it, simply standing under the sheer gray face of the rock gave me shivers. But our guide assured us we wouldn't be climbing at the peril of our lives. To protect ourselves, we'd wear a "belaying line." This was a rope thrown down from the top and wound around our waist, then knotted securely over our navel. At the top, a large, strong, and very alert person kept a firm hold on the rope. As we climbed, he took up the slack, not so much to pull us, but just enough to catch us quickly if we slipped.

Imagine your temptation like climbing a rock face. God's at the top, holding the belaying line. He gives you just enough slack to let you climb freely and creatively. But He also keeps a tight hold so that if you fall, you won't tumble all the way to the bottom and smash into bits.

That's real freedom. What kind? Freedom from fear, because you know God will catch you. Freedom to express yourself creatively as you climb the wall. And freedom to know God intends that you ultimately will succeed.

That's His promise as we face temptation. Victory is a choice, yes. But it's also a guarantee as we walk with the Lord. He gives us real relief every step of the way.

BATTLE WEAPONRY

WHAT YOU GOTTA KNOW

CHAPTER 12

The Japanese attack on Pearl Harbor goes down in history as the "day of infamy." But it was also probably the greatest sneak attack of all time. Years of planning, study, and intelligence operations preceded that momentous day, December 7, 1941.

In fact, one of the ways the Japanese learned about the ripe moment for attack was through a unique intelligence operation. Whenever Japanese citizens traveled to the U.S., they were questioned on their return about American habits and lifestyle. Through these interrogations, the Japanese military came to an incredible conclusion: the most vulnerable moment for American troops was 7 A.M. on a Sunday morning. Why? Because Saturday night they went out on the town, drank, and lived it up. Come Sunday, they had hangovers, slept in late, and if they went anywhere, it was to church. They certainly weren't thinking about attack!

Any strategist will tell you that the gathering of intelligence—information about your own forces and those of your

120

enemy, as well as the terrain and climate in which you will fight—is the key to victory. Often the one who knows more wins, even if he leads inferior forces.

Now that we're about to describe our actual weaponry against temptation, the first piece we need to study in our minds is knowledge. Do we know ourselves? Our God? Our enemy? Our weapons and their weapons? The times and places in which we'll be fighting?

The more we know and the better we tap that knowledge in crucial moments spells the difference between making wise choices and foolish ones, choices that lead to victory and those that lead to defeat. What then do we need to know?

KNOW YOURSELF

"Know thyself," Socrates emphasized to his students. Awareness of both our weaknesses and strengths, our up-and-down times, and the moments when we're apt to be vulnerable strengthens us in a multitude of ways. If we wage a constant battle against eating too many sweets, then we need to recognize that a stroll down the candy aisle in the local supermarket can be lethal. We should decide to avoid it. If we're single and we know that reading a big sexy novel before bed will inflame our lust, then we must veer away from those books at those hours (or stop altogether). If we know that a surge of buying lust strikes everytime we saunter into the mall, maybe we shouldn't go there as often. Or visit it without credit cards and take only the cash necessary for planned purchases.

It's your basic game of "if it's not there and I can't get it, I won't be tempted." Satan generally tempts us only with real possibilities, not with things we know we cannot get, buy, borrow, beg, or steal within minutes.

When you know and understand yourself, you can begin dealing effectively with the temptations that assault you. Ask these questions:

1. What are my most difficult temptations?
2. When do they strike?
3. Why do they strike at that time and place?
4. Why am I so susceptible to these temptations and not others?

5. Are there steps I can take to defuse tempting situations before they arise? Are there ways to avoid them, or eliminate them?

As we isolate answers to these questions, we begin to learn that there are strategies we can use to stop temptation. For instance, if we discover that certain activities "feed" and stoke the desire for something we know is sinful, then why not take steps to stop feeding those desires? If potato chips are your downfall, why not keep them out of the house? Then when temptation strikes at 10 P.M., there's simply no way to fulfill it without a special run to the store. If rock music saps your spiritual energy, get rid of all your rock tapes. Then when temptation hits, there'll be nothing to listen to! If Sarah and Jeannie constantly tempt us to gossip, why not say to them, "Please pray with me that I'll stop gossiping"?

KNOW YOUR SINFULNESS

"Two Gun" Crowley was at one time one of New York's worst and most dangerous criminals. One night a policeman walked up to Crowley's parked car where he was necking with a girl and asked for his license. Crowley said nothing, but pulled a gun and shot the man till his gun emptied. Then he jumped out of his car, pulled the policeman's own revolver, and fired one more round into the man's skull.

Later that night, police gathered around his apartment, firing fusillades to force him into surrendering. Crowley returned the fire, but somehow found time to write a blood-stained note. It said, "Under my coat is a weary heart, but a kind one — one that would do nobody any harm."

As he sat in the electric chair at Sing Sing awaiting execution, he said, "This is what I get for killing people? No, this is what I get for defending myself."

Al Capone, Chicago's "Public Enemy Number One," once said, "I have spent the best years of my life giving people the lighter pleasures, helping them have a good time, and all I get is abuse, the existence of a hunted man."

Dutch Schultz, New York City's mobster, called himself "a public benefactor."[1]

---

[1]Dale Carnegie, *How to Win Friends and Influence People* (New York: Pocket Books, 1964), pp. 20–21.

What did these men have in common? They failed to see their own sinfulness.

Christians likewise can think "more highly of themselves than they ought." Next to Al Capone, Dutch Schultz, or Two Gun Crowley we may think we're pretty fair examples of decency, but our byword should be, "There but for the grace of God go I." Any of us, if given complete freedom and power to do as we please, would certainly abuse that power to the pain of all concerned. Lord Acton (1834–1902) said, "Power tends to corrupt; absolute power corrupts absolutely." For God, this is not true. But in the case of man and angel, it's absolutely true. We behave no worse than when everything and everyone goes our way. We will inevitably take power to the limit and beyond, if we can.

The fight against temptation is one in which we must all recognize our innate sinfulness. Without God's grace, every one of us is on the road to murder, adultery, thievery, rape, pillage, plunder, prostitution, and every other sin in the alphabet. It's only His restraining goodness that keeps any of us from plunging off the precipice into complete debauchery.

"Not me," one says. "I'm not that bad."

Only because God hasn't let you become that bad.

"But I have convictions and beliefs. I know what's right."

And what's wrong. And you'd prefer the wrong if the Lord hadn't transformed your mind.

"I would never do such a thing."

Maybe not that one. But there's always something!

It doesn't much matter how the devil gets us. One sin is as good as another. The road to hell is paved with good intentions, small compromises, and tiny departures from truth. He moves us along a millimeter at a time. But in the course of a year, those millimeters can stretch into spiritual kilometers.

As we reckon with our sinfulness, we open the way to getting help. Only when we admit we cannot go it alone will we ask Him to come along with us. Only when we see we cannot win without His power will we reach out for His hand.

KNOW YOUR FATHER

J.I. Packer has written that the purpose of life is "knowing God." He's right. The Westminster Shorter Catechism asks,

"What is the chief end of man?" Answer: "To glorify God, and enjoy Him forever." It's through knowing God that we learn how to defeat sin. The closer we draw to Him, the closer He draws to us and the more we resist the devil (see James 4:7-8).

Treasury Department agents who investigate counterfeiting of American money do not study fake bills. Rather, they scrutinize real money until the pattern is so imbedded in their minds they can instantly recognize any departure from it.

We learn to defeat sin not by looking the devil in the eye, but by fixing our hearts, minds, and souls on Christ. Martin Luther once demonstrated to his students the source of his dog's obedience. He threw a bit of meat on the floor and commanded the dog not to move. What did the dog do? He didn't look at the meat; rather, he riveted his eyes to his master's face without a blink. Luther made the application: We defeat sin not by staring sin down but by looking to Jesus.

As we settle our minds on the truths and realities of our Father's love, goodness, steadfastness, and forgiveness, we begin to find greater freedom from sin.

While teaching a class in my church on temptation, I followed the outline of this book. One of my lessons, covered in chapter 2, spoke of how Satan uses temptation to lead us into sin and make God look bad. While talking to one of the members of the class, she told me, "You know, that principle has helped me tremendously. I realized that when I sin, I'm not only hurting myself — which, to my shame, doesn't bother me as much — but I'm also hurting God and His reputation. That made me think. I'm finding that I resist sin all the more because I don't want to shame the Father and make 'the Gentiles blaspheme.' "

It became a potent insight. I realized the power there is simply in knowing the Lord is with us wherever we are. While filling out expense booklets, tax returns, and other financial statements, I'm often tempted to hedge. However, I've found through tough experience that when I have cheated, the Lord convicts me so deeply that I have to go back and correct the mistake. Now when I'm tempted, I'm already thinking, "If I do this, the Lord's going to convict me and I'll have to go back and fix it. That will mean more time, more money, more effort, and even a little embarrassment on my part." So I figure I'll just do it right the first time.

KNOW YOUR BIBLE

The best way to put together a model is to follow the directions. The fastest way for Dad to get the boy's bike to work on Christmas Day is not to wing it, but to follow the manufacturer's steps to the letter. You want to get from here to there? Get out a map and figure out the best route. Don't decide, "I'll just wait for the inspiration to hit me."

When it comes to temptation, though, few of us follow the recipe. We turn to the Bible, if we turn at all, only as a last, final, and unwilling effort. Even then we may not like what we find and try something else.

But the Book offers us the first, best, and easiest solutions to many tempting problems. Who has not struggled with escalating arguments and hot words with a spouse? How do we keep things from detonating? Proverbs 15:1 has a ready answer: "A gentle answer turns away wrath, but a harsh word stirs up anger." Yet, some husbands and wives go for years without learning about the Bible's "gentle answer."

Tempted to complain about an unreasonable boss? First Peter 2:18 has a word of advice: "Slaves, submit yourself to your masters with all respect, not only to those who are good and considerate, but also to those who are harsh."

Fighting off a spirit of bitterness about a setback? Consider two words from 1 Thessalonians 5:16: "Rejoice always." Then verse 17: "Pray without ceasing." And finally verse 18, "Give thanks in all circumstances."

The Scriptures don't provide specific answers about everything. Medical problems can't be solved by memorizing a few verses. Nor will a quarterback find instructions in its pages on the shotgun formation. But on the subject of temptation we can be sure it provides some strong and stark lessons. We must learn to apply our will to Scripture's wisdom. The words are there, but we must make the choices.

I have struggled over the years with a repeated craving for rock music. Sometimes it's a nice way to relax. But often it's just a waste of time. I used to turn on the radio the moment I hopped into the car. I've found that I cannot defeat the desire simply by telling myself no. Several methods, though, have helped. Instead of listening to whatever comes on the radio, I carry a number of tapes — speaking tapes, some Christian music, as well as some selected secular musicians whom I consider neutral or at least safe. I use these as substitutes for the preferences of past years: Led Zeppelin, the Rolling Stones, and Jethro Tull. By finding worthy substitutes, my desire diminishes.

But even more effective and God-honoring is meditation on Scripture. I try to spend much of my forty-five minute commute to and from work reviewing books of the Bible in my mind. Through that discipline I've memorized many books of the New Testament and gained an in-depth knowledge of Scripture and the Lord behind Scripture. It has become the greatest weapon in facing temptation. It tells me the truth at any critical moment. It offers insight about how to solve problems. It encourages me in the tricks of battle. And it shows me the way around, through, over, or under.

KNOW YOUR ENEMY

Paul's words in Ephesians 6:12 ring the warning knell for Christians. "Our struggle is not against flesh and blood, but against the rulers . . . of evil in the heavenly realms." While the flesh introduces powerful suggestions into our minds and the world places transfixing images before our eyes, it's ultimately the devil who longs to fell us. As we begin to understand Satan's strengths and weaknesses, liabilities and limits, we can anticipate better the time, place, and direction of battle with him. Much of this book has looked directly at his talent for deception, seduction, and argumentation. Being aware of his voice inside our minds becomes a potent weapon of perseverance.

During my years in seminary, I had a professor named Walter Baker who taught missions with a zeal I had never seen in a missions instructor before. I had long regarded missions with guilt and confusion. I worried about it constantly. Then during one class, Dr. Baker challenged us to write down all the reasons we *didn't* want to be missionaries.

It was an intriguing thought. Yet, as I sat down to list my

well-intended complaints the fog only seemed to increase. Guilt showered down like sleet and I felt cold and alone.

I stopped one afternoon before the assignment was due and sat in the class amphitheater praying, thinking, and wondering over this nagging problem. Finally, I said, "OK, Lord, You are not a God of confusion but of peace. Help me to see my way clear on this." I began to write as I asked the question, "Why don't I want to be a missionary?" In the end I listed over seventeen reasons. Several of them went like this:

1. I don't want to get killed by being shot with arrows.
2. I don't want to have to eat sweet potatoes and squash all my life.
3. I can't live without air-conditioning.
4. I don't want to have to wear people's hand-me-downs.

As I looked over the list, I almost laughed. Was this what was troubling me? I took the list to Dr. Baker. He looked over the list and responded, "First of all, you will not be shot with arrows. More than likely, they'll use an Uzi. Second, missionaries do get goat meat now and then too. Third, if what you refer to as air-conditioning is what I've experienced in the U.S., most of it is broken down half the time. And fourth, as for the hand-me-downs, you really ought to take a look at what you're wearing now."

He made me laugh. But I realized how Satan had hoodwinked me. His weapon was darkness, confusion, disorientation. A little light, a little truth, and his fog dissipates. I have not become a missionary to darkest Africa as I once feared, but I have found a strong mission field right in my neighborhood and workplace. Sometimes your friends and coworkers are the most difficult of all to convert. But I have to admit I still do prefer air-conditioning.

KNOW YOUR RESOURCES

Besides the Bible and God Himself, there are a multitude of resources God gives us to ward off the power of temptation. What are they? Think of just a few:

The Spirit of God—Paul said, "Live by the Spirit and you will not gratify the desires of the sinful nature" (Gal. 5:16).

Other believers—enlisting their prayer, by confessing your sins and being accountable to them.

Healthy diversions—substituting godly activities for the ungodly or worthless.

Counselors—those who are paid to offer biblical advice, and those who function as spiritual mentors.

Books, videos, and tapes—they remain a source of inexpensive and enlightening insight.

The church—certainly an important source of comfort, encouragement, help, counsel, and fellowship.

Small groups—your small group can be one of the best sources of help, wisdom, and uplift.

A mentor—someone whom you trust and can confide in about anything on earth.

Specific texts, quotes, and principles you have stored in your mind—whatever you've memorized to recall in a critical moment are like David's five round stones used to fight Goliath; your finest and readiest weapons.

Meditation and prayer—you can practice these anywhere, anytime, and retreat to that special place in your soul where you can hide and talk with God about anything.

All these resources function as our best weaponry in the war for righteousness.

KNOW YOUR STANDING

As a final help in the battle, we must recognize our standing before God. He loves us, will never forsake us, and promises to be our guide, friend, refuge, and strength in all the byways of life. There is no sin He cannot forgive, no problem His wisdom cannot untangle, no difficulty His insight cannot see clear. So long as we go to Him, call on Him, rely on Him, walk with Him, there is nothing to fear.

A realistic comprehension of our standing before the Lord brings with it immense power and confidence. I tested it out even tonight as I went by a local shopping center to pick up a pizza. I was about thirty minutes early and walked about praying. The air was frigid; it had snowed eight inches the day before. As I rounded a corner, a tall black man stopped me and asked, "Sir, could you take me out to Route 108? My car broke down."

I reflected a moment, stifling the fear that this could be some kind of setup. I said, "Sure, where do you live?" He told me, we went to my car, and I drove down the road toward his home. The whole time my mind kept shouting at me, "Watch out. This guy is setting you up. Just wait till you get out in the dark somewhere."

We talked. He worked in a local detention center as a maintenance man, had seven kids, two in the military. We discussed the economic situation and the possibility of war in Saudi Arabia. Meanwhile, the road got longer and darker. We kept getting farther and farther afield, when he finally told me to turn left, then cried, "Why, there's my brother now!" The truck ahead of us, apparently, contained his brother.

Now I knew it was a setup. A dark back road. This man in my car. His brother in the truck ahead of me. But suddenly something else came into my mind. "He can't touch you, Mark. God is with you. God is ruling in this world. He can't do a thing to you unless God allows it." I sarcastically added, "That's what worries me — what God might ALLOW!"

But my knowledge of God's sovereignty, goodness, and power stayed my soul. The fear disappeared, and I simply enjoyed his talk about his children, the church, and his life. Finally, I dropped the man off without an incident. He thanked me and proceeded to try to sell me 10 of his 103 acres. I declined and was on my way. I realized God gave me a chance to use my extra thirty minutes that night for His glory.

Knowing where we stand with God will dispel the fear Satan fires into our minds in a temptation situation. As you repeat the words of Psalm 23 in your mind, or a passage like Romans 8:28 or Philippians 4:6-7, the truths of the Scriptures stoke the coals of spiritual fire in our hearts. We find the grit and muscle to face the challenge without wavering. Temptation is no longer an overpowering bully. No, victory becomes a choice we can make everytime.

PUTTING ON YOUR SPIRITUAL ARMOR

CHAPTER 13

Alypius, a friend of St. Augustine, the fourth-century theologian and writer, scorned and hated gladiatorial contests. He refused to enter the arena. But one day his friends forced him inside against his will. He resolved not even to open his eyes at the spectacle. However, a piercing cry from the arena floor aroused his curiosity and he opened his eyes just a crack. Seeing a stream of blood pouring from a victim's side, he gazed on in astonishment. As the combatant succumbed to the thrust of a sword, the crowd roared. Moments later, Alypius felt his own blood surge and joined with them, shouting out bloodcurdling screams in response to the battles going on before his eyes. In a short time, he not only became a willing and enthusiastic supporter of the contests, but he encouraged his friends and acquaintances to join in with him.

Paul echoed in Romans 1:32 the response of Alypius: "Although they know God's righteous decree that those who do such things deserve death, they not only continue to do these very things but also approve of those who practice them."

One of temptation's greatest problems is not just giving into it ourselves; but having launched into the sin with abandon, we also begin clapping the backs of those who join with us. We become "sin evangelists," exporting our vices and persuading others to join us.

How do we break the cycle of sin and start living free and godly lives, committed to God's righteousness? Paul gave us the answer in Ephesians 6:13-18. In that passage he lists the hardware of spiritual warfare, the armor we're all to wear as we engage in spiritual combat. The passage reads,

> Therefore, put on the full armor of God, so that when the day of evil comes, you may be able to stand your ground, and after you have done everything, to stand. Stand firm then, with the belt of truth buckled around your waist, with the breastplate of righteousness in place, and with your feet fitted with the readiness that comes from the Gospel of peace. In addition to all this, take up the shield of faith, with which you can extinguish all the flaming arrows of the evil one. Take the helmet of salvation and the sword of the Spirit, which is the Word of God. And pray in the Spirit on all occasions with all kinds of prayers and requests. With this in mind, be alert and always keep praying for all the saints.

What is this magnificent array of spiritual protection and weaponry? Undoubtedly, as Paul wrote the Letter to the Ephesians he scrutinized the armor that each of his personal Roman captors wore. He was imprisoned in Rome, under house arrest. He was probably chained to one guard wrist to wrist. Perhaps another stood at his doorway, fully equipped.

As Paul penned the letter, he pictured the spiritual warfare that he and all Christians engage in. It occurred to him that Roman armor offered an excellent analogy for what he wanted to convey.

TRUTH

The first thing he noticed was the belt that girded the Roman's waist and loins. The soldier tied this on first. The girdle anchored all the other pieces of armor because they were attached to it, including the scabbard for the sword. The genius of the Roman armor was that the girdle gave the soldier complete freedom of movement. He was not hampered by anything clanging or swinging at his side. No part of the armor threatened to pull off so long as the belt girded him tightly. Just as the sprinter "dressed down" to a minimum amount of clothing so he could run without hindrance, so the Roman soldier dressed up in a minimum of armor that would both protect him perfectly, yet leave him free to fight with complete skill and precision.

What did Paul mean by the "belt of truth"? Is it the truth of the Gospel, the whole body of truth we find in Scripture, or just truthfulness — speaking with integrity and honesty?

All truth really is grounded in God's truth. As we gird ourselves with the truth of God as recorded in Scripture, all the effects of truth come with it: honesty, integrity, truthfulness, and a rejection of falsehood, lying, deceit, and trickery. In other words, we're not just to fill our minds with biblical truth; we're to let it affect what we say and do. The person girded with the belt of truth will speak the truth when asked. He will shun the little tricks used to deceive his coworkers, friends, and neighbors. He will speak up about Christ when an opportunity presents itself and not tell himself he's a "silent witness" or that "his life is the witness."

How does this help in the war against temptation? Truth enables us to see that sin leads to death, pain, guilt, and loss. We recognize deceit for what it is. While looking good up front and promising an immediate reward, in the end we see that deceit results in destruction. We tell ourselves the "truth" about sin. We never sugarcoat it, or say it's "just a small vice." We don't excuse sin because "everyone has their foibles," or because "God will forgive us afterward." No, we bring complete honesty to everything we do, never hiding our sin when we commit it, and avoiding wrongdoing the rest of the time.

Martin Luther said, "A man's beard is like original sin; although we daily destroy its manifestations, it constantly reappears."

The girdle of truth helps us admit the problem, confess our

sinfulness, and learn to depend on Christ and His people for help. We know sin will pop up again tomorrow. But we press on, resolving to use truth to light the darkness.

RIGHTEOUSNESS

The second piece of armor is the "breastplate of righteousness." It was typically a single piece fitted to the contours of the soldier's chest and abdomen. It protected the inner organs from a sword thrust, arrow, or spear. Preachers and theologians argue whether this piece of armor refers to Christ's righteousness, which God imputes to us at salvation, or personal righteousness and holiness of living. The answer is that it can refer to both. Christ's righteousness protects us before God's wrath. Because He has clothed us in Christ's perfections, we need not fear any condemnation from God. Thus, though the devil may accuse us before the Almighty, we know that He remains with and for us.

On the other hand, God said, "Be holy, because I am holy" (1 Peter 1:16). When people accuse us of sin, saying, "I'm righteous before God" carries no meaning. No Christian can use his justification in Christ to excuse sin (see 4:12-19).

Rather, the holiness of God transforms us into people who practice righteousness in all of life. Practical goodness—living a good, clean, and decent life—carries weight and power with non-Christians as well as Christians. It's a protection against accusation and the blasphemy of others. When we are accused, Peter warns us that "doing good . . . will silence the ignorant talk of foolish men" (2:15). He says earlier, "Live such good lives among the pagans that, though they accuse you of doing wrong, they may see your good deeds and glorify God on the day He visits us" (v. 12).

Clearly, God has in mind a twofold righteousness—the perfections of Christ that protect us from guilt and condemnation before God, and a life of actual righteousness—that keeps us from guilt before others. Either way we are strengthened, and the devil cannot attack our conscience.

PEACE

Paul calls the sandals the soldier wore on his feet—the third piece of armor—the "readiness that comes from the Gospel of peace." The Roman donned hobnailed sandals to gain firm footing in hand-to-hand combat. If an enemy soldier knocked him to the ground, he became completely vulnerable to attack from all directions. But sandals that offered firm footing as well as ease of movement became an excellent and important weapon.

We see again a twofold purpose in the sandals: firmness and quickness of movement. What do these sandals represent in the battle against temptation?

Nothing less than an ability first to stand firm on the basis of the peace we have in Christ, and second, the power to run circles around our enemy in the sweat of battle. God's peace in the Gospel gives us both fearlessness and forthrightness. We know we have the truth. We know it can't be taken away. Therefore we become bold in facing temptation. We don't succumb to it. We know God is with us and on our side. Next, we become direct and honest in confronting sin. We don't hedge. We call sin and temptation by their right names. We don't pretend it's just a foible or a personal idiosyncrasy.

FAITH

The shield of faith, the fourth part of our armor, was the large, body-length shield a Roman soldier placed in front of him to ward off fiery darts. Often their enemies threw darts whose tips were wrapped in a yarnlike cloth and dipped in pitch, then set on fire. The Roman shield, covered with leather and soaked in water before battle, extinguished the dart's flames. It enabled him to march on his adversary and duel him in hand-to-hand combat where the darts were useless.

What then is this shield of faith? Clearly, it's that plain and steadfast reliance on God that His truth can snuff out any accusations, temptations, deceptions, or tricks of the devil. Faith in His Word extinguishes the flames that threaten to ignite us into lust, anger, malice, or illicit desire. As we place our trust in His promises, He destroys the power of temptation.

Marilyn Andreres, a writer, mother, and homemaker, told me about her struggles as a young Christian. "Early on," she said, "I was tempted in not believing the divinity of Christ. Then I was tempted to unbelief in my own salvation. Then it turned to more specifics in my life—unreasonable fears, jealousy, and envy over others' possessions and ministries. After twenty years of knowing Christ, my temptations now fall more in the area of perseverance—not wearying in well doing."

What helped her? For her early temptations it was "simply getting into the Word and finding out what it said." For fear she found strength in the words of Psalm 42:5: "Why are you downcast, O my soul? Why so disturbed within me? Put your hope in God, for I will yet praise Him, my Savior and my God." Envy about others' possessions was gradually extinguished as she concentrated on Scriptures that talked about being a "co-laborer with Christ" (see 2 Cor. 6:1; 1 Thes. 3:2). Through faith she destroyed "the flaming darts of the evil one."

She also told me that she believes many Christians face temptations that are aimed at undermining the truths of Christianity. That is not to say that Christians are not tempted in the ways that unbelievers are. That would be naïve. But below I list some areas where I've seen this premise at work:

The Truth of Christianity	How Satan Tries to Weaken This Truth in Believers
1. Our salvation is a gift of God's grace.	1. We try to earn salvation and criticize the performance of self and others.
2. Jesus is Lord and Savior.	2. We live practically like atheists, not believing He can help.
3. Only through God can we live righteous lives.	3. We live as though we don't need Him.
4. God is personally accessible.	4. We don't believe that His nearness will do us good.
5. His Word—nothing	5. We don't revere His

added or deleted—is our authoritative guide.	Word or use it as we should.
6. Developing relationships with others is a prime way to show our love for God.	6. We treat relationships carelessly.

Her idea is sound. Only faith can destroy these missiles of Satan.

HELMET OF SALVATION

The fifth piece of armor, the helmet, protected the skull and brain. It's our most vulnerable and indispensable body part. Paul calls this protecting piece the "helmet of salvation." This headgear refers not only to the actual salvation we have in Christ, but to all the security, confidence, hope, and assurance that comes with it. If we have no sense of safety and certainty in our destiny with Christ, we will run from battle every time. Why fight? We could lose our lives.

But with a knowledge in our hearts that salvation is ours, we can stand up to any enemy, knowing that death is only the passageway to everlasting life with Him. Struggle is only a means by which we grow stronger. Setbacks are only opportunities to live for Him all the more.

THE SWORD OF THE SPIRIT

Paul speaks of the "sword of the Spirit" as the "Word of God." The Romans had a short sword that was double-edged and ideal for close combat. It could be whipped out for fighting in moments. The soldier could cut with both sides, making it especially lethal. And it was small enough so as not to tire the fighter in a lengthy duel or hamper him when warriors grappled closely.

What a wonderful picture of the power of the Word of God! Hebrews 4:12 speaks of God's Word as "sharper than any double-edged sword," penetrating "to dividing soul and spirit, joints and marrow; it judges the thoughts and attitudes of the heart." The Spirit takes the Word and convicts the world of "sin and righteousness and judgment" (John 16:8). That is, through the Word God points out a man's sin, demonstrates his lack of righteousness, and assures him of his accountability. He stands convicted, overwhelmed, and ready to sink to his knees in repentance.

Of course, the Word of God doesn't always appear to have this effect. Many people hear it every Sunday and go away unmoved. But who knows what lurks in the hearts of men? Even as a non-Christian, I remember the conviction I felt when confronted with a message from the Bible. I didn't understand why at the time, but in the face of Scripture all my rationalizations were incinerated. I wouldn't admit that to anyone. Nor would I show the least fear on my face. But deep down the Word struck. It does the same with both believers and unbelievers. They may pretend that it means nothing. But God strikes at the very heart.

In a battle with temptation this means that God's Word is our best and most formidable offensive weapon. Jesus' quotation of Scripture three times during Satan's test in the wilderness should be enough to convince us that even God incarnate relied on the Word to send the devil packing.

David Bauer, the manager of a greenhouse and a husband and father of four children, related the power of Scripture in his personal battle with gossip and laziness. "A lot of times I just tell myself a truth like 1 Corinthians 15:58 that I'm to be diligent, or 1 Corinthians 10:13 that there is a way of escape. I tend to rationalize things. I tell myself I have four kids, I shouldn't need to get that involved in church. When I come home I'm tired. I work a physical job. But then I think of that 'way of escape' idea. I can get real judgmental with people, feeling they may be doing something wrong. Then I'm constantly critical and not loving the way I should. 'Do not judge lest you be judged' helped a lot."

Years ago, he used to watch with his family a TV show called "Barney Miller." "My kids were four, five, six years old. They'd be there with me as I watched the show. Some of the language on it was bad. Not as bad as movies and things. But I realized I wasn't sure young kids like that could understand and handle it without using the same kind of language. I kept thinking about the Bible's words about not using 'obscenity, foolish talk or coarse joking' (Eph. 5:4)—so I just stopped watching the program. The fact of the Word and what it said had power. It gave me the determination to follow through."

The Word is a sword. It cuts away the thick net of sin that Satan lays over and around us. It carves a clear path for the walk ahead.

PRAYING IN THE SPIRIT

Paul calls the final weapon prayer. Some would say this isn't a distinct piece of armor. But in a way, it's the most important. A soldier needs to communicate with his commanding officer as well as listen for his orders. Prayer is that communication.

Some Christians stumble on the phrase, "praying in the Spirit." They believe this means some mystical brand of prayer, speaking in tongues, or the "groans too deep for utterance" mentioned in Romans 8:26-27. But Paul illuminates the meaning in the following verses: "Pray in the Spirit on all occasions with all kinds of prayers and requests. With this in mind, be alert and always keep praying for all the saints. Pray also for me, that whenever I open my mouth, words may be given me so that I will fearlessly make known the mystery of the Gospel" (Eph. 6:18-19).

The word "prayer" involves every sort of communication with God—praise, petition, entreaty, thanksgiving, supplication. "Requests" are any specific item we want God to provide—for ourselves, the church, a friend, or anyone else. Obviously, Paul wants us to pray in our native tongue so that we understand what we're asking for. Praying in the Spirit refers simply to "Spirit-led" petition as John instructed us in 1 John 5:14-15: "This is the confidence we have in approaching God: that if we ask anything according to His will, He hears us. And if we know that He hears us—whatever we ask—we know that we have what we asked of Him." Jesus put it this way: "If you remain in Me and My words remain in you, ask whatever you wish, and it will be given you." Paul also makes the connection of being "filled with the Spirit" (Eph. 5:18) and letting the word of Christ "dwell in you richly" (Col. 3:16).

Clearly, praying in the Spirit is praying according to God's will. All that involves is taking the truths of Scripture and turning them into prayer, because that is His will.

I find this a particularly powerful truth. Frequently, if I find myself struggling to know what to pray about, I open to a passage of Scripture and "pray through" it. If you're studying 1 Corinthians 13, ask the Lord to make the love Paul talks about a reality in your life. Ask Him to enable you to be "patient, kind, not jealous, not boastful, etc." Pray the same thing for your church, your family, your friends and neighbors.

In a specific situation of temptation, find a Scripture that relates to the problem and pray to the Lord that He'll give you the power to live out that verse. If your problem is dirty language, like what David Bauer was bothered by, pray through Ephesians 4:29: "Lord, help me not to let a 'putrid word' come from my lips; rather enable me to speak 'what is good for edification' and respond to 'the need of the moment' so that I can 'give grace to the one who hears.' " If your difficulty is lack of compassion, turn to Colossians 3:12: "Help me, Lord, to put on a heart of 'compassion, kindness, humility, gentleness, and patience.' Show me the way to be forbearing and forgiving and how to 'put on a heart of love.' "

This prayer can be done with virtually any passage. It's just a matter of choice and commitment.

SOLDIERS

Like it or not, we're soldiers engaged in battle. Like Paul told Timothy, we can't get "involved in civilian affairs" because we want "to please our commanding officer" (2 Tim. 2:3-4). A soldier doesn't charge into battle naked and vulnerable. He wears armor, comes with a sword, and obeys orders.

I've always enjoyed the words of Billy Sunday. "I'm against sin. I'll kick it as long as I've got a foot, and I'll fight it as long as I've got a fist. I'll bite it as long as I've got a tooth. And when I'm footless, and fistless, and toothless, I'll gum it till I go home to glory, and it goes home to perdition."

Winston Churchill's words thrilled me when I read them for the first time in a book of speeches: "We shall not flag or fail. We shall fight in France, we shall fight on the seas and oceans. . . . " I could almost hear his raspy, English voice enunciating every word. "We shall fight with growing confidence and growing strength in the air, we shall defend our island, whatever the cost may be. . . . " Whatever the cost? Absolutely. This was life or death!

"We shall fight on the beaches, we shall fight on the landing grounds, we shall fight in the fields and in the streets, we shall fight in the hills. . . . " I could see the soldiers standing, firing, falling. But as each one succumbed, another stood to fill his place and take back lost ground.

And then that final thundering clause: "We shall *never* surrender."

Never in a million years. Never in this life. Full steam ahead. We shall not surrender. We shall triumph by the power of the blood of the Lamb, who has made victory sure and secure.

Our attitude toward temptation and sin requires the same ruthlessness that Patton brought to his battles with Rommel, the same determination that Sunday brought to his preaching, the same commitment that Churchill stoked when he defied Hitler. Never surrender! No quarter! It's war to the finish.

CUT THE CORD

CHAPTER 14

Franz Kafka (1883–1924), the Czechoslovakian writer and existentialist, once said, "In the fight between you and the world, back the world."

Many Christians could easily identify with that thought. The modern church and multitudes of believers today can make a disturbing identification with the seventh church that John describes in Revelation 3. Laodicea was "neither cold nor hot," but lukewarm, worldly, wealthy, yet poverty-stricken spiritually. It's not the world around us that's troubling, but the world in us. Few modern saints can resist the tantalizing lure of material plenty so available to most of us. We play the lottery in hopes of gaining more. We max out our credit cards so we can stash a few more goods in the home. Our lives are in constant motion—from video store to restaurant to movie house to dance hall. As one bumper sticker puts it, "I owe, I owe, it's off to work I go."

What exactly is worldliness? It's more than what you do; it's who you are inside. Two Christians might attend the same party, movie, play, or eatery. Both might appear very similar in all respects. Yet, one could be worldly, the other sold out for Jesus. How do you tell the difference?

It's demonstrated most by the way we talk, think, make decisions, and treat others. It's not simply by whether or not we indulge in one or two of the "nasty nine," "filthy five," or "dirty dozen" sins. When a young man asked Jesus to divide an inheritance between him and his older brother, Jesus responded rather hotly. "Who made Me a judge over you?" He went on to speak about greed and the fact that one's life does not consist of his possessions. Then He gave His questioner a powerful picture: a farmer who builds bigger and better barns only to be called a fool by God. Why? Because he stored up "things for himself but [was] not rich toward God" (Luke 12:21).

Worldliness is the attitude that leaves out God, forgets God, pushes God aside, or pays Him public lip-service for the sake of image. The worldly person becomes self-indulgent, looking at everything in relation to how it will advance, help, encourage, and strengthen him. He forgets ideals. He strips himself of all vestiges of inner life, calling it a "waste." He disdains religion, faith, and commitment to a calling as "foolishness." Amassing wealth, building a reputation, gaining awards and prestige, these are the things that matter to him. He concerns himself with style, image, fashion, self-promotion, and self-gain. And the only individual that ultimately matters is himself.

AXIOMS OF THE MODERN WORLD

I once heard Dr. Howard Hendricks spell out ten "axioms of our culture," the basic values that the worldly person holds to. They are:

1. Values are relative. There are no absolutes. You determine what's "right for you." Obviously, Christians can do this as much as non-Christians. IMPLICATION: No one can claim to know the absolute truth on any issue.

2. What can't be proved can't be believed. If you can't see it, then it's not real. Science is God. IMPLICATION: You can believe in God, but you'll never be able to prove His existence, so don't make such a big deal about it.

3. Scientific knowledge is certain. "The findings of modern science" are utterly reliable. Stake your life on it. IMPLICATION: Only science can tell us the truth.

4. There is no evidence of the existence of life after death; therefore, live it up now. Though this notion is changing because of the investigations of recent death experiences, the idea that there is no real accountability beyond this world seems to be the guiding principle. IMPLICATION: No one has to worry about being judged for his sins.

5. Real is what can be seen and handled and sensed. The spiritual is a waste of time. Again, this idea is changing, especially with some of the New Age propositions, but many still cling to it. IMPLICATION: Spirituality is nice, but it's not real, so don't give your life to it.

6. Man is insignificant, just a little speck. When you're old and useless, why keep on living? IMPLICATION: You don't matter that much; therefore what you do doesn't matter either — to God or anyone else. So live it up now.

7. I cannot help being what I am; I am the product of my environment. So don't blame me for my sins. IMPLICATION: Don't expect me to change or apologize for my errors.

8. Freedom means doing as I please. Don't restrict me in any way. Restriction is the ultimate immorality. IMPLICATION: Don't fence me in! Get rid of all these little laws. I want to be free.

9. To be certain about religion is arrogant. To proclaim that you know "the truth" or "the way" is the height of pride and conceit. IMPLICATION: Don't take religion too seriously.

10. The laws of nature determine everything. You can't avoid them, so work with them. Life is ruled by deterministic forces. IMPLICATION: The survival of the fittest is the name of the game.

Go through those ten axioms and consider the implications. Is your life being guided by such principles? Are you living according to these ideas even though you might not wish to if you thought about it?

A POTENT PASSAGE

A helpful passage of Scripture on the subject of worldliness is found in 2 Corinthians 6:14-16. Paul says, "Do not be yoked together with unbelievers. For what do righteousness and wickedness have in common? Or what fellowship can light have with darkness? What harmony is there between Christ and Belial? What does a believer have in common with an unbeliever? What agreement is there between the temple of God and idols?"

Paul says we are not to be "yoked together" with unbelievers. Frequently, this passage is used to guide Christian single people in dating and marriage. It is a caution that they are not to marry people of a non-Christian faith.

But in reality, while the principle pertains to marriage, Paul's intent reaches much farther than that. The words "unequally yoked" are used only one other time in Scripture, in the Septuagint version of the Old Testament. In Leviticus 19:19 Moses commands the people not to "mate different kinds of animals." It appears to be a warning against placing together unlike animals, such as an ox and a horse or jackass, to plow a field. The purpose, obviously, was to avoid unnecessary pain on the part of the animals as well as possible hostility.

What does this illustration have to do with the unbelieving world? Paul uses "unequally yoked" to mean a situation in which you become "mated" or "joined" to someone in a way that leaves you in a weak, subservient, or "unequal" position. In other words, you put yourself into a legal, marital, or emotional contract that could force you to submit to habits or practices that the Bible condemns. This can happen in five areas.

Morality. "What do righteousness and wickedness have in common?" Paul's obvious answer is "nothing." Righteousness is all that conforms to God's person, character, and law. Wickedness is anything that departs from it. The world sucks believers into its system when they shed basic biblical morality for the world's ways. National issues like abortion and euthanasia and personal choices in so-called "gray" areas like movies, videos, drinking, drugs, reading material, and so on are all affected for the worse.

The way of wickedness has coaxed and beckoned the naïve since the beginning of time. Tablets in the Museum of Constantinople, dated hundreds of years B.C., record the lament,

"We have fallen upon evil times and the world has waxed very old and wicked. . . . Politics are very corrupt. Children are no longer respectful to their parents."

Edward Gibbon's classic history *The Decline and Fall of the Roman Empire*, published in 1787, isolated five causes of Rome's decline. They were: 1. The rapid increase of divorce; the undermining of the dignity and sanctity of the home which is the basis of human society. 2. Higher and higher taxes and the spending of public money for free bread and circuses for the populace. 3. The mad craze for pleasure; sports becoming every year more exciting and more brutal. 4. The building of gigantic armaments when the real enemy was within: the decadence of the people. 5. The decay of religion—faith fading into mere form—losing touch with life and becoming impotent to guide the people.[1]

Arnold Toynbee echoed Gibbon's comments: "Out of 21 civilizations preceding this one, 19 of them have been destroyed by a mixture of atheism, materialism, socialism, and alcoholism."[2]

Anything that weakens commitment, faith, and love for God qualifies as a "moral" issue. Some Christians may enjoy a risque movie, while for you the images conjure difficulties with lustful, bigoted, or hateful thoughts. One believer can read Danielle Steel with no spiritual effect (or so he or she says), while another cannot peruse that material without compromising basic convictions and conduct. Anything that promotes wickedness, makes it attractive, tolerable, or just interesting, is worldly. The world's way is to cross God's fences and stray as far into demonic territory as possible, all the while proclaiming, "There's nothing wrong with it." Paul warns us not to be deceived. Righteousness and wickedness have nothing "in common." No common goals, priorities, convictions, beliefs. Therefore, do not mix the two.

Guidance. "What fellowship can light have with darkness." I call this the issue of guidance. Where do we seek counsel, help, direction, advice—in the light, or in the darkness? The "light" side offers insight, purpose, thoughtful illumination. It

---

[1]Paul Lee Tan, *Encyclopedia of 7700 Illustrations* (Chicago: Assurance Publishers, 1979), p. 250.

[2]Tan, *7700 Illustrations*, p. 250.

exposes falsehood. It makes plain the errors of what might appear benign and neutral.

Darkness on the other hand obscures, shadows, and cloaks the consequences of its pleasures. It tells us, "Come along. There's no harm. It's just a little fun." But what it really asks is that we step off the twentieth story of a firmly founded building into the empty space of immorality, impurity, sensuality, and the like. There is no hope but that we'll eventually plummet to the ground, a so-called victim of our own stupidity.

Satan's greatest weapon is darkness. Keeping things hidden from those who would detect his pitfalls insures his victory. But when the light shines, the truth becomes clear. This is why the forces of darkness make such an effort not only to ridicule the truth, but to hide it, extinguish it, eliminate it altogether.

Brenda Diana Duff Frazier Kelly Chatfield-Taylor started life with millions in her pocket. A debutante at age 17, she dated John F. Kennedy and became engaged at one point to Howard Hughes. She was "Glamour Girl No. 1" of New York society. She died at age 60 in May 1982, but not before summing up her life in an epitaph. She commented bitterly of her high-society experience: "All it brought me was despair."[3]

General Omar Bradley described our age with these sobering words, "The world has achieved brilliance without conscience. Ours is a world of nuclear giants and ethical infants."[4]

Service. "What harmony is there between Christ and Belial?" In other words, how can Christ and the devil hope to work together? They can't. One can most easily pinpoint worldliness by whom we serve: Christ, or the world, flesh, and devil. If our lives become meaningful and tolerable only when we indulge ourselves in the world's pleasures, we have reached the upper limits of dissolute living.

Does church work and service bore you? Is there little interest or personal sense of reward from what you do in the

[3]*Time,* May 17, 1982.
[4]Quoted in *Leadership,* Winter 1980.

name of Christ compared to the "joys" of this age? Would you rather attend a party or watch "Monday Night Football" than visit the sick, help someone in need, show a kindness, give a gift? Some even mock the question: "You make Christianity sound completely boring! Why can't we enjoy 'Monday Night Football'?" The point is, you can. But is that the best use of your time and talents? Is that the way God would have you spend it? When we have gotten so saturated in worldliness that the question even seems impertinent or foolish, perhaps we have reached a point of no return.

In a humorous vein, a psychotherapist counseled a female patient in her mid-twenties. She complained of nervousness, saying life was too hectic. Just "too many big weekends, too many discos, too many late hours, too much talk, too much wine, too much pot, too much lovemaking." The therapist commented, "Why don't you stop?" The patient appeared dumbfounded, until insight flooded her eyes. "You mean I really don't have to do what I want to do?"[5]

Whom do you serve—Christ or Belial?

Truth. "What does a believer have in common with an unbeliever?" This relates to the issue of truth. The worldly shun, laugh at, compromise, water down, evade, rationalize, and eventually annihilate the truth. They cannot bear the presence of truth at all. Truth exposes error. This is why the Scriptures are so powerful in confronting an errant world. God has invested each statement from the Bible with His own life. It pierces to the heart. It unveils sin. To sin in the face of truth becomes impossible without feelings of guilt, anger, or rebellion, which expose the sinner all the more.

The world assaults Christian beliefs continually. It longs to excise them completely from society. Right now the attack is mounted against all vestiges of religion in government. But obviously books, history, private business, the church, and the home are next. The world will not be content till all traces of another "way" are erased.

John Bunyan once wrote in "A Caution to Stir Up to Watch Against Sin,"

---

[5]Cited in *His*, October 1981.

Fools make a mock of sin; they will not believe
It carries such a dagger in its sleeve.
How can it be, they say, that such a thing
So full of sweetness should ever wear a sting?
They know not that it is the very spell
Of sin, to make men laugh themselves to hell.

The world weaves a spell, assuring us sin possesses no sting, injects no poison, delivers no death. The spell is broken only when we lie gasping on the way to hell's gates, wondering what happened, how we could have been so foolish.

Worship. "What agreement is there between the temple of God and idols?" The fifth area the worldly attack is worship. They seek to replace God with idols, worship with entertainments, prayer with human assertiveness, and praise with platitudes. When worship becomes a drudgery, a mindless hour of tedium at the end of an otherwise eventful week, something has gone wrong.

The church was never meant to compete with the latest videos. Emotions stamped onto celluloid and delivered to the eyes and mouths of eager watchers seem much more interesting than the "psalms, hymns, and spiritual songs" that Paul speaks of. The moment a pastor begins to "preach" we tune out, seeking out a quiet place in the soul for thoughts of worldly plans, like whether the roast beef is cooking properly, or if Jane will say yes to Billy on this week's soap.

Yet it's also true that the church has fallen behind in providing cogent, honest answers to today's seekers. Pastors pass over the Bible for more "up-to-date" ideas because they feel the Scriptures are neither relevant nor communicable. But if we gave the same amount of time to making the Word of God plain and easy to understand as we do to shaping a joke or illustration, we might find our audiences much more receptive. Some of the world's most renowned preachers today are men who make God's Word their focus. The world, however, tells us that we need something more appealing to reach today's masses.

Two old myths are helpful illustrations. When Homer's Ulysses passed the Isle of the Sirens in his ship, he wanted to hear their mystic music without jeopardizing his life or crew. He filled the ears of each sailor with wax so they could not hear. Then he lashed himself to the mast. As a result, he passed safely by the shore of the sorceresses without harm.

However, another great warrior, Orpheus, used a different method. While searching for the Golden Fleece with the Argonauts, he also passed the Sirens' isle. Orpheus was endowed with supernatural musical ability. It was said that when he played, animals and even rocks and trees moved about him in dance. As they neared the evil Sirens, Orpheus took up his lyre and played so beautifully that the crew sat entranced and jubilant in its sounds, paying no attention to the Sirens!

In a sense that is God's response to the world. He makes the music of heaven so beautiful that none will want to dance to the tunes of earth.

The committed Christian must make a choice to cut the umbilical cord that joins him to the world. Once done, that commitment will be tested over and over as the world conjures up new pleasures and devices to lure him away. But as he turns to the Lord, he finds that what He offers in terms of genuine joy, real love, lasting peace are so potent that the world can do little to compete.

Still, it comes down to a choice. Will I follow the world, or God?

Dwight L. Moody was once asked, "Mr. Moody, I want to be a Christian, but must I give up the world?"

Moody replied, "Young man, if you live the out-and-out Christian life, the world will soon give you up."

As a spring tree sheds the last dead leaves of autumn by pushing the new sap up into the branches, so the Christian eventually cleanses himself of the world by letting the Spirit fill him. He'll soon find the world will either be attracted to salvation or repulsed because of its sinfulness.

John Wesley once said, "Give me a hundred men who will hate sin and nothing else, and fear God and nothing else, and I will change the world."

Unfortunately, it seems Wesley is still looking for his hundred. But you and I are available right now. What choice will we make?

LOOK FOR THE ROUTE OF ESCAPE

CHAPTER 15

The movie *Raiders of the Lost Ark* is one of those action thrillers which, despite its terrible theology, still excites me even though I've seen it numerous times. What I like most about Steven Spielberg's masterpiece is that Indiana Jones repeatedly falls into traps and circumstances that leave the viewer guessing, "Good grief, how is he going to get out of this one?" Trust Indiana to find the reckless, breath-stopping route out every time. And he does it with a sheepish grin and a little shrug, "Ah, it was nothing."

Sometimes I think of God as the master movie director of an epic in which each of us has a major role. He plans to put us into every death-defying, mind-boggling, heart-banging circumstance until the moment when everything seems to be lost, and then He assures us He'll always supply the fast exit out—if we want it.

That's the essence of the passage we find in 1 Corinthians 10:13: "No temptation has seized you except what is common to man. And God is faithful; He will not let you be tempted beyond what you can bear. But when you are tempted, He will also provide a way out so that you can stand up under it."

REALIZE YOU'RE NO DIFFERENT

The above text is crucial for anyone who wants to walk with Christ and overcome the power of temptation. A man named Frank I discipled years ago began a memory verse program, and that passage became the first Scripture verse he ever learned. Early on in his Christian life I feared that because he'd been an alcoholic, he would go back to his old ways. What concerned me most was his statement that he'd "always been a good man." Frequently he assured me that though he'd been a drunk, for the most part he was "decent, loving, and a Christian." He told me how he volunteered to clean a local church as a young father, and how he'd served consistently. I impressed on him the sinfulness of man and our helplessness apart from Christ. Though he agreed verbally, he always seemed to believe in his innate "goodness."

Then I urged Frank to memorize more Scripture. One morning as we studied the Word together, he suddenly said, "Mark, I've been studying this stuff for a while now, and you know what? I'm learning I'm not such a good fellow after all. It seems everywhere I go now, the Holy Spirit reminds me of little things I'm doing wrong. I have to change."

We began going through the Old Testament together, but for a period I couldn't attend our morning sessions. I was worried that Frank and his wife might stop their studies. One morning I called up to see how things were going. I knew they should be in the middle of Leviticus and felt sure they'd be bogged down. But when I called, Frank was excited. "All those laws, Mark. It's amazing me. They had to do this. They had to not do that. Did you know those people couldn't eat crabs?"

Coming from a dyed-in-the-wool Marylander, that was close to blasphemy. I laughed and said, "That's right, Frank."

"And ham too! They couldn't eat bacon. Boy, am I glad I was saved in the twentieth century instead of in the time of Moses."

Boy, was I glad too. It struck home to me again the power of God's Word. It reaches us in ways no human words can express.

Notice what Paul begins his promise with: "No temptation has seized you except what is common to man." In other words, nothing we face is unique. Men and women through the ages have fought the same battles. It's only Satan's lie that deceives us into thinking no one anywhere else has ever experienced what we're going through.

Realizing you're not unique and that the temptations you battle are "common" changes attitudes. One, it tells us we can't use the excuse that our situation is different from those of other people. Two, it means that others are a sure source of understanding and help, because many of them have struggled with the same things. Satan's best weapon is to keep Christians away from one another. If he can halt our "gathering together" then he'll also tell us not to "confess our real sins" because "people will think poorly of us for it." While confession of sin in public should be entered into carefully and tactfully and probably only among those we trust, it has intrinsic spiritual power. When we expose sin, we encourage the possibility of healing. But when we hide our sin, like an untreated cancer it only grows and defeats us.

RELY ON GOD'S FAITHFULNESS

The second thing Paul says is to rely on God's faithfulness. For one thing, God limits temptation: He will not "let you be tempted beyond what you can bear."

Ultimately, that's a wonderful promise and a stark piece of accountability. It guarantees that nothing we face is unbearable, intolerable, too great, too much, or comes at a time when we're too weak. Jesus languished at His weakest point in the wilderness, yet Satan could not dislodge Him from His conviction. We can be sure that no matter how powerful or appealing a temptation seems, God will prevent it from exceeding our endurance.

One of my respondents told me how he sometimes battles the temptation to sleep in on Sundays and not go to church. "It seems I'm always up late the night before and then in the morning I'm wiped out. But I found a way out." What was it? "When the alarm goes off, I turn it off. But if I'm tempted to get back into bed, or reset the alarm, I just pray, 'Jesus, You handle this while I go take a shower.' I don't know why that works, but somehow it gives me the gumption to do what I know is right."

No matter how tired he feels, he says, he knows that's only part of the deception and the appeal of the sin. He tells himself God has limited the temptation. Once he takes that shower he'll feel all right.

Cliff Rapp, a pastor in Southern California, told me how a woman asked him for marriage counseling. He wanted to avoid the situation entirely. "Satan tried to discourage me," he said. "He gave me all kinds of excuses to avoid getting involved. 'You don't know how to do this kind of counseling.' 'You're too busy to get involved.' 'If you stick your nose into this, her marriage will blow up and everyone will blame you for the divorce.' "

What did he do? "I prayed and trusted that God was in this and would give me the power, knowing that Jesus is greater than the tempter, my inabilities, and that lady's problems. I went ahead with the counseling, and the Lord gave relief to the lady."

If we cannot believe in God's sovereignty and lordship over our lives and the temptations we face, then most of the promises in Scripture, most of the grand commands and assurances of grace, are empty. God can't do anything to help us.

But if His promises are true—and they are—then we can face temptation boldly, knowing that He has already gone before us, letting through only that limited parcel of evil that He knows we in His grace can overcome.

This truth carries with it great responsibility. It means we cannot ever say, "I was tempted beyond what I was able to handle." Yes, it probably felt that way. And if we've habituated ourselves to a sin—drugs, alcohol, overeating, lack of discipline, unrestrained anger, jealousy—the cycle will be hard to break. But this promise covers even that situation. With all the tools God has given us, we can win through making the right choices, even though they may hurt.

HE LEADS US THROUGH

God is also faithful in leading us through temptation. The text says He will "provide a way out." It's the classic escape hatch. Yet, this isn't a token loophole or empty promise. With any temptation God provides a real, honest way of escape that honors Him.

Two famous illustrations that come to mind are the experiences of Eric Liddell and Corrie ten Boom. Liddell's 100 meter heat for the 1924 Olympics was on a Sunday. He believed he should not break the command to keep the Sabbath. So he refused to run, even though that race was his best event and many had slated him to win. He might have felt that God had dashed his hopes. But instead, he prepared for the 200 and 400 meter dashes secretly. He won the bronze medal in the 200. But it was the 400 meter race that made him a legend. The judges placed Liddell in the far outside lane, the worst location for running such a race. He ran the first 200 meters at a blistering pace. Everyone was sure that in the second half he'd "blow up" or crumple in agony on the track, having spent his last wind. But instead, Eric gained ground on his contenders, running in his wild, arm-waving, head-back style. He set an Olympic record that stood for many years. He was the first Scotsman ever to win a medal.

God showed him a way of escape and glory.

Corrie ten Boom tells the story of how her family hid Jews from the Nazis in her native Holland. While visiting some relatives, they became aware of a trap door for hiding the young men of the house that was located under a rug in the kitchen. A table was kept on top of the rug, but they all knew it was far from adequate protection.

Then one night a "razzia" occurred. These were the lightning-like raids German soldiers made on Dutch homes to find young men to work in the German factories. Before the Germans burst in, the two boys were able to get inside the hole under the table, and the women covered it back up. But being a Christian household, the young people all believed strongly in never telling a lie, no matter how justified it seemed at the time.

As the soldiers searched the house, the guards addressed Cocky, one of the children. They demanded, "Where are your men?" She explained about Corrie and the others, but the soldier was impatient and repeated the question. Corrie wondered, "Would she lie? Could she lie? But if she didn't, they would find them."

Cocky stalled further by explaining that the older boy was off at school. The soldier roared, "What about the other two?"

Corrie relates that Cocky didn't miss a beat: "They're under the table!"

She'd done it! She'd told them where the boys were. But when the soldiers lifted up the tablecloth, everyone laughed as if it were a joke. The soldiers were furious and stomped out.[1]

This isn't a treatise on ethics or lying. I for one would not have hesitated to lie to a criminal like that to legitimately protect someone — the laws of God are higher than the laws of men in such a case. And yet, God gave them a route of escape. It's remarkable, yet true.

ROUTES OF ESCAPE

What are some scriptural routes of escape?

Run. Joseph fled from Potiphar's wife. Paul counseled Timothy to "flee the evil desires of youth" (2 Tim. 2:22). There's nothing wrong with running in the face of strong temptation, whether it's running away, running from one book to another, running from one room to another, or simply running in your mind to think on something else. Physically leaving the source of temptation, though, is an excellent method.

Much of Jim Elliot's personal thoughts are recorded in Elisabeth Elliot's book, *Shadow of the Almighty*. A girl named Evelyn Corkum wrote down something Jim had said about boy-girl relations: "Don't put yourself in a position to see how good your resistance is. When you feel temptation coming, get out of there!"[2]

There's no special pride in standing and falling when your attacker is a tempter.

Resist. James says, "Resist the devil, and he will flee from you" (James 4:6). The word for resist means to "oppose" or "array yourself in battle against." In a real battle, there can be no ambivalence. You win only when you decide that noth-

[1]Corrie ten Boom, *The Hiding Place* (Old Tappan, N.J.; Fleming H. Revell Co., 1971), pp. 90–91.

[2]Elisabeth Elliot, *Shadow of the Almighty* (Grand Rapids, Mich.: Zondervan, 1958), p. 120.

ing less than winning will satisfy. You can never win if in your mind you fight a second battle that says, "Should I or shouldn't I?"

The key to resisting the devil is single-mindedness. Any doubt, any sense of "Yes, I like what you're saying, but I really shouldn't . . . " brings the house down. When we resist him, though, leaving no room for a pull in the other direction, he will flee.

Sing and rejoice. In Acts 16, Paul and Silas lay in a bug-ridden dungeon in chains. They must have been tempted to despair. But God gave them a route away from dark thoughts: through song, praise, and prayer. They sang wholeheartedly. That singing drove out all the feelings of fear, the lack of resolution, and doubt they might have otherwise harbored.

I always liked the scene in the movie *Casablanca* where the Nazis crowd the French locals away from the piano. They begin raucously singing some offensive Nazi songs that put the Frenchmen into a stunned and angry silence. But suddenly one of the heroes gets the band to strike up "La Marseillaise." In moments, the whole crowd joins in singing the French national anthem and the Germans are drowned out.

A good song not only can lighten up a desperate situation but also inundate the flames of sin within. It takes your mind off your troubles and reminds you of the greatness and power of God.

Confront. Frequently, the "way of escape" is not an escape at all, but a direct confrontation. Nehemiah squared off with Sanballat and Tobiah as they ridiculed the Jews who were rebuilding the walls of Jerusalem. He couldn't run from the temptations they hurled at him in the form of taunts, threats, and laughter. So he confronted them with a trowel in one hand and a sword in the other.

Similarly, Jesus couldn't run from the tempter in the wilderness, but replied to each taunt with sober words of Scripture. Satan withered in the confrontation and ultimately left. I earnestly believe the devil and his cohorts cannot bear to hear the words of Scripture from the lips of one committed to obeying them.

Substitute. Many times the way out is to substitute the temptation with a legitimate activity. Daniel and the three

Hebrews in Babylon requested that they not defile themselves with food from the king's table. They were given a trial period of ten days to eat food of their choice. When it was discovered at the end of that time that they were even healthier than the other trainees, they were allowed to continue.

You can substitute a craving for potato chips with something else: taking a walk, eating raw vegetables, going for a drive, listening to a tape, watching a video. You might confront a problem with lust at nighttime by substituting exercise earlier in the day to make you tired, by a refusal to feed your lust by avoiding things that encourage it, and by listening to praise music or spending time in the Word.

The key to a worthy and effective substitution is that:

a. It must be truly enjoyable to you.

b. It must take you away from the temptation.

c. It must be given time to work.

Don't expect that a substitute will provide the "magic answer" immediately. But with practice and effort, it can become a powerful method of escape from temptation.

Call on the Lord. The first thing Moses did when he wanted to give up was call on the Lord. Gideon cried out for God's help in leading Israel against the Midianites. Samson found the way out by returning to God. All through Scripture we see a recurring record of a person who prayed and a God who answered.

Don't make the mistake, though, of praying on Sunday for crop failure when all week you've sowed wild oats. And don't ask God to "take away the desire." He usually won't if you ask in a pinch. But over a period of time, through using the tools, practicing godliness, growing in grace, we will be able to see change.

Dr. William Backus writes in his book *Finding the Freedom of Self-Control* that we can rarely expect God will give us instant self-control. Often Christians find that early in their walk with Christ a multitude of habits and sins fall away with barely a whisper of prayer. Backus tells how he was "released from every trace of the desire to smoke tobacco"—a habit he'd been enslaved to for over twenty-five years. The same thing happened to him with alcohol.

But then, he says,

> God did not in that same instant give me painless, effortless success in controlling everything. Other domains of behavior remained difficult to gain control over. Results came much more slowly. . . .
>
> In fact, after working with hundreds of fellow Christians to help them gain control over behaviors which were controlling them, after hearing their stories and carefully gathering the facts, I have concluded that God often works in just this way: He bestows self-control instantly in answer to prayer in a few areas, but deals with many other self-control problems by deliberately enlisting us in a daily struggle.
>
> God purposely steers us into battles we *can* lose (though our ultimate victory is His responsibility), shows us where the weapons and armor are kept, and then allows us to try our mettle, never leaving nor forsaking us, but not stepping in to take over the conflict *for* us.[3]

The miracle of God's providing the ways of escape for us is that He leaves us intact, completely ourselves. He never turns us into robots. He never forces our hand or puts a gun to our back to command us to live a certain way.

Tim Stafford gives an effective example in *Unhappy Secrets of the Christian Life*. He tells how the submarine *Thresher* went too deep under the North Pole and collapsed under the weight of the water. It was crushed into tiny bits in the ensuing implosion.

The pressure we see in deep-sea diving can be like that pressure we feel in temptation. To dive deep a nuclear sub needs thick steel bulkheads to take the squeeze of the water. But such subs have limited capabilities. To get down into the lowest places, scientists are lowered in heavy steel balls created especially to take the intense pressures of the deep sea.

---

[3]William Backus, *Finding the Freedom of Self-Control* (Minneapolis: Bethany House, 1987), p. 34.

But lo! What does the researcher find down there? Fish. Little bug-eyed monstrosities. You'd think these little creatures would be built like M1 tanks. But they're not. Only micrometers of skin cover them. Why? Because as Stafford says, "they have a secret: an equal and opposite pressure inside themselves."[4]

The way to deal with temptation is not to retreat from the world, load on bulkheads of steel, and hide somewhere in the dark, terrified of the pressures outside. No, get an "equal and opposite" pressure inside you: the power of the Spirit, the Word, the Father, and the weapons of our warfare.

---

[4]Philip Yancey and Tim Stafford, *Unhappy Secrets of the Christian Life* (Grand Rapids, Mich.: Zondervan, 1979), pp. 24–25.

BE ACCOUNTABLE

CHAPTER 16

There's a story about a psychoanalyst who tried to cure a female kleptomaniac. After many sessions, the analyst announced the woman was cured. "I really am?" she cried with joy. "Absolutely!" the analyst assured her. "I believe the problem is under complete control. You can go out into the world and live like anyone else."

She hugged him. "I'm so happy. I don't know how I'll ever repay you for your help."

"My fee is all the payment I expect," the analyst said with a smile. "However, if you do happen to have a relapse, you might pick up a video camera for me."

So much for psychoanalytical cures. Yet, much sadder stories are true. On March 9, 1981, Stephen T. Judy was electrocuted in Indiana for raping a young mother and murdering her and her three preschool children. Judy had spent most of his life after age thirteen in jail. He testified at his murder trial that he couldn't "control himself" and committed twelve to fifteen rapes while in high school. Ultimately, Judy claimed that America and society had failed him. Shortly before his execution he said, "Doing all the small crimes I did was my crying out, saying, 'Stop me, something is wrong.' If society is not ready to help or correct people like me, then they might just as well go ahead and do away with us."[1]

On August 18, 1988, a .38 caliber bullet ended the life of a Washington State Superior Court Judge, Gary Little. Prior to his suicide Little had committed a long string of homosexual seductions of teenage boys and juveniles in his courtroom. Little's friends and associates knew about his liaisons and reports were even filed. But the state's Commission on Judicial Conduct suppressed them. As early as 1985, reporters for a local TV station had wanted to air a story about the judge's activities. But the station's programmers killed the story. Finally, on the night of August 18, 1988, the Seattle *Post-Intelligencer* informed the judge it would publish the story of his secret life in the next morning edition. The judge shot himself later in the evening, leaving a note that said, "For me, it is an appropriate end to the present situation."[2]

What is the common thread in these two stories? Accountability, or the lack thereof. In each tragedy, a man's sinful failure was in some respects a failure on the part of those around him. They should have called him to account for his crimes.

THE GREATEST PROBLEM

For many Christians, a "besetting" sin is the bane of their existence. My interviewees have told me of long-term problems with anger, jealousy, adultery, masturbation, lying, stealing, dishonesty, lack of personal discipline, and a multitude of other sins that have left them, at times, unable to speak. One man spoke of homosexual deeds as a youth that still haunt him. He is nearly forty-five years old. Another man mentioned affairs and the temptation to get involved again, defying all reason, experience, and counsel. He couldn't seem to stop himself. The books I have read and articles I've checked also refer to difficulties both contemptible and incomprehensible. Yet, they were all expressed by average Christians,

[1]*The Baltimore Sun,* March 9, 1981.
[2]*The Washington Post,* October 30, 1988.

people far from reckless savages or wanton criminals.

What is the answer to such problems?

We can choose to sin, or we can choose to trust, obey, and submit. That second choice, though, seems to some a matter of insurmountable difficulty. The inner drive that propels some of our temptations into sin overwhelms us. Before it we are as matchsticks in a hurricane.

Mark Chapman, who shot and killed the former Beatle, John Lennon, battled an inner impulse that seemed to overwhelm him. His former pastor, Charles McGowan, said Chapman overcame the compulsion a short time before the actual crime. But after returning to Hawaii with his wife, Chapman "stayed there two or three weeks and the drive began to build up in him again. . . . He said he lied to his wife and borrowed some money and slipped out of Hawaii without telling her where he was or what he was going to do, and flew back to New York."[3] There he shot and killed John Lennon.

"Bobby" Matta recently made headlines as the murderer of three Washington, D.C. prostitutes. He grew up in a home that practiced a variation of the Sikh religion, and his upbringing caused him to feel tremendous guilt following sexual acts. Voices spoke to him in such a way that he "had an irresistible impulse to obey command hallucinations," according to his lawyer, R. Bronson Levin.[4]

What is this impulse, this force inside of us? In Matta's case it could certainly be demonic. Others appear to be fighting their own sinful nature. For all of us, though, the process is the same. The first impulse strikes, an idea is planted, a desire arises, we stoke and build the feeling with our own agreement, and soon it rages into a fire out of control. The place to stop it is when it's just a tiny flame. It's then that we still have control.

But how do you get control?

THE POWER OF ACCOUNTABILITY

Becoming accountable to others is the crucial point of hope for many. James counseled his readers, "Confess your sins to

---

[3]*The Baltimore Evening Sun,* January 29, 1981.

[4]*The Washington Post,* December 12, 1990, p. B5.

each other and pray for each other so that you may be healed. The prayer of a righteous man is powerful and effective" (James 5:16).

Confession of sin frees. It gives one assurance about God's forgiveness. But it also does something else: it makes you accountable.

James didn't want us to stop at confession and go no further. He meant, "Keep on confessing your sins and keep on praying." In other words, choose people around you whom you trust and make them your confessors, mentors, and prayers. By going public with your sin, you get a double victory. One, cleansing; and two, someone who will ask you if you're keeping to the straight and narrow, especially if you ask them to do that very thing.

Contrary to Cain's outburst about Abel's whereabouts, we are our brother's keeper. We are called constantly to confront, discipline, win, and restore Christians caught in sin. Jesus told His disciples it was their responsibility to go to a sinning brother and lead him to repentance (Matt. 18:15-17). Paul repeatedly warned his readers to restore those who have sinned (Gal. 6:1), to admonish one another (Rom. 15:14; 1 Thes. 5:11-14), to put out unrepentant sinners (1 Cor. 5:1-8), and to have nothing to do with those who do not respect the commands of Scripture (2 Thes. 3:14-15). James says that "if one of you should wander from the truth and someone should bring him back, remember this: whoever turns a sinner from the error of his way will save him from death and cover over a multitude of sins" (James 5:19-20).

But what if the person "caught in a fault" goes to his brother before being confronted? What if he preempts it all by saying, "I need help. Make me be accountable to you"?

A PERSONAL TESTIMONY

I have found the power of accountability to other godly people a mainstay. Recently, when I took a leave of absence from my company, I discovered an incredible problem. My newfound freedom resulted in a sudden departure of good habits, namely waking up early and staying up all day. Since my computer was in the basement, all I had to do was stumble out of bed any time I wanted and go to it. Soon I was going to bed at 4

A.M. and waking up at 2 P.M. My schedule became hideous. The idea of having to meet someone early in the morning produced near-seizures. I was stupefied and ashamed.

No matter what I tried, it didn't work. Setting a louder alarm, praying about it with more fervor, even getting my wife to help me did nothing except aggravate everyone. My time, like it or not, was my own.

But I didn't like it. Then I hit on two ideas. The first was to take on the responsibility of getting my daughter to school each morning. That made me get up. The idea of having to explain to her teachers that she was habitually late because her old man was a lazy slob truly intimidated me.

The second step was even better. I meet with a group of businessmen every Friday morning at 6:30 for prayer, Bible study, and fellowship. (True to form, I often stayed up the whole night on Thursday so I wouldn't have to wake up too early Friday morning.) I finally cast off my pride and told them my sin. I asked them to hold me accountable about my hours each Friday, and "to demand" a specific day-by-day breakdown.

Was I amazed! The idea of having to tell seven or eight respectable Christian businessmen, doctors, and dentists that I'd slept in till 2 P.M. nearly gagged me. I got my act together fast. I still slipped now and then, but when they popped the question each Friday morning with eyes blazing, I knew I had better shape up.

I'm not saying that becoming accountable will cure all problem sins, but it's a start and a help. Just the idea that some important Christian may ask me how I'm doing with my wake-up discipline stirs me to action in the morning. Accountability also encourages me to have regular devotions. Mark Twain cut to the heart of the matter when he said, "There are several good protections against temptation, but the surest is cowardice." Just knowing someone will ask you about how you fared last week against your pet sin might give you the willingness to choose rightly.

What should you look for in a spiritual confidant?

1. Decisiveness. He can't patsy around with you. He must mean business.

2. Determination. He must keep at the problem until you say it is gone.

3. Dependability. You must know that he'll always raise questions about that troubling sin. If he doesn't, you'll always be hoping for an escape.

4. Dedication. He must also pray for you, as well as hear your sins.

5. Deference. He must respect you in spite of your sins.

6. Distinction. He must also be a person of character himself and one you feel you can trust.

If you find a man or woman like this, don't let him or her go. You've found a jewel who may help you grow like never before.

When I worked as a pastor, I frequently had prayer with families at the church early in the morning. One kid named Justin who came in mentioned that he and his little brother Timothy were always fighting. He wanted to pray about that, so we did. Then I asked him if there was anything else. He said, "Well, one thing is that I'm always teaching Timothy nasty words to say and nasty things to do, and I don't think that is right. So pray that I won't do that anymore." The next morning he came in all smiles and informed me, "I didn't teach Timothy one nasty thing yesterday."

Accountability and prayer work in tandem. Even for the youngest of God's children.

KEEP GETTING UP

CHAPTER 17

Socrates said, "It may be that the Deity can forgive sins, but I do not see how." Henry Ward Beecher had another thought: "A forgiveness ought to be like a canceled note, torn in two and burned up, so that it can never be shown against any man."[1]

William Penn put it this way: "If I am even with my enemy, the debt is paid; but if I forgive him, I oblige him forever."

Ann Landers said, "One of the secrets of a long and fruitful life is to forgive everybody everything every night before you go to bed."[2]

Perhaps William Arthur Ward said it best. "Forgiveness is a funny thing. It warms the heart and cools the sting."[3]

When Abraham Lincoln was asked how he intended to treat the Southerners once they were defeated and returned

[1]Quoted in *Homemade,* July 1981.
[2]Quoted in *Reader's Digest,* September 1980.
[3]Quoted in *Reader's Digest,* April 1980.

to the Union, he replied, "I shall treat them as if they had never been away."[4]

Certainly these remarks provide a glimpse of how to understand God's forgiveness. While our purpose is to live holy lives and summarily defeat the tempter in his attempts at leading us into sin, there will be times when all of us fall. Few of us can terminate a pattern of sin without an occasional blunder or mistake. Fewer still will live unstained lives that all will call "blameless." Perhaps the greater problem for those who are tempted is not how to win, but how to survive after they've lost. Guilt can crush us. Remorse can lead us to weariness of soul. Or we can go in another direction altogether and dismiss it all very lightly, saying, "God will forgive; that's His job. So I needn't worry if I sin."

Both attitudes are out of balance. We cannot react to our personal sins either with profuse recriminations or wanton shrugs of the shoulders, as though to say, "Oh, well, I did it again. So what?"

What then is the proper and biblical attitude toward sin and our failure as Christians?

RECOGNIZE THERE ARE CONSEQUENCES

First and foremost, we must recognize that sin brings consequences. Occasionally, God obliterates all the personal results of sin; we're pardoned, and it feels as though we can start life over with a clean slate. After receiving a pardon from Gerald Ford, Richard Nixon faced no immediate consequences or prison term for his role in the Watergate coverup. However, his friend Chuck Colson did go to prison, even though he had repented not only before man, but before God.

Abraham suffered no apparent bad results for his lies to Abimelech and the King of Egypt about Sarah being his sister. In fact, in each case he seemed to gain in power and wealth. That's a rare instance. More typical was the fate of King David, who after sinning with Bathsheba, found his life in turmoil. Though God forgave him, He also said He would pay him back fourfold for his deeds.

The Scriptures record a multitude of stories of sin and

---

[4]Donald L. Bubna with Sarah M. Ricketts, *Building People* (Wheaton, Ill.: Tyndale House, 1978), p. 135.

consequences, even though in many cases there was genuine forgiveness extended. Start at the beginning with Adam and Eve, go next to Cain and Abel, the world before the Flood, the Tower of Babel, Samson and Delilah, Eli and his errant sons, most of the kings of Israel and Judah, Peter, Judas Iscariot, and a multitude of others—we see the grim results. God forgives in many cases—if we repent; but He rarely mitigates the worldly results of our conscious and premeditated transgressions.

This was pressed home to me again as I read Allan Emery's story collection called *A Turtle on a Fencepost*. He tells the story of Charlie, who was a habitual liar as a teenager. Though his parents disciplined him, Charlie kept on lying. Finally, his father, a farmer, told him, "Charlie, every time you tell a lie I am going to put a nail in the barn door."

Strangely, Charlie liked the idea; it wasn't as bad as a spanking. A single nail was hardly noticeable. But in no time dozens of them covered that door. Everyone asked what it meant, including visitors, relatives, and the local pastor. Charlie's father quietly explained they were a record of his son's lies.

After a whole month of this, Charlie had had enough. He told his father he'd never lie again. Then he said, "Will you take the nails out?" His dad answered that if he did not lie for a whole month, he'd remove them. Thirty-one lieless days later, Charlie's father pulled all the nails. But as Charlie stood back to look at the nail-less door, his joy turned to tears. "The nails are gone but the marks are still there!" he cried. Charlie's father reminded him that while God's forgiveness was complete, the consequences of the sins still remain in our lives until death.[5]

What a picture! It says it all. The sins are gone, but the marks remain. Even God's forgiveness cannot always erase the results of our sin. They're a reminder that while we're acceptable forever and can never lose our pure standing before Him, we didn't get that way on our own efforts. Only Christ's sacrifice will ultimately eliminate every remembrance of sin once His kingdom begins.

---

[5]Allan C. Emery, *A Turtle on a Fencepost* (Waco, Texas: Word Books, 1979), pp. 21–22.

FORGIVENESS COSTS

A second thought we ought to imbed in our hearts is the fact that forgiveness cost God the life of His Son. Sometimes people wonder why Christ *had* to die. Wasn't there some other way? Socrates' words quoted at the beginning of this chapter expose the problem: How can God forgive, if He is to remain just and righteous?

Man's sin presented an impossible dilemma for God. If He simply forgave us by a verbal decree, His standards of justice and holiness could not be met. If He sends us all to hell the moment we sin to satisfy that justice, His love and grace become an impossibility. Within His own breast rages the contradiction. He wants to forgive, but He cannot compromise His holy character and righteous indignation at sin. He wants to punish, but His love, grace, and kindness cry out for reprieve. What can He do?

It's all solved in the cross. By taking a sinless man/God and punishing Him in our place, He made it possible to extend to us His forgiveness. But in order to claim it, we have to accept what Christ did in our place. Otherwise, forgiveness remains beyond our reach.

When we accept Christ we receive all that God offers in Christ: forgiveness, heaven, eternal life, an inheritance, perfect righteousness.

All those gifts, however, come at great cost to God Himself. Forgiveness is free, but it's not cheap. Someone had to pay to make it possible. God made that payment with the life of Jesus Christ.

TWO KINDS OF FORGIVENESS

There are two different kinds of forgiveness. One is God's eternal forgiveness that we receive at salvation. This was what He referred to when He said He "blotted out" our sins (Isa. 44:22), cast them "into the depths of the sea" (Micah 7:19), and separated them as far as the "east is from the west" (Ps. 103:12). He doesn't "remember" these sins, according to Isaiah 43:25 and He has put them "behind His back," as Isaiah 38:17 says.

God has obliterated all record of our sins — past, present, and future — from all minds and hearts. When we stand before

Christ at the Bema judgment seat, He will not bring up any dirty laundry to show off to the gathered billions. He will not read off a list of infractions and chuckle over them at a "saint roast" somewhere down heaven's road. He won't feature special cinematic events in which our lives on earth will be shown on giant heavenly screens for all to gloat over.

No, God's forgiveness is final, irrevocable, and complete. No sin will be left unforgiven. We will not have to purge ourselves in a purgatory or "wait in line" for release from limbo. Salvation burns the record to nothingness. It's gone, wiped out, judged, paid for, over and done. Forever.

Nonetheless . . .

There's always something, isn't there?

Yes, nonetheless, a second kind of forgiveness relates to fellowship and communion with God on a daily basis. While there's no condemnation for daily sin (Rom. 8:1), there is separation in a spiritual sense. Feelings of guilt cloud our mind when we commit acts we know God hates. Fear of exposure or of God's anger can keep us from praying, going to church, walking with God the way we should. When we're practicing sin, we don't feel right in God's or others' presence. We need to confess such sins so that we can be "healed" (James 5:16). That healing refers both to physical and spiritual health. A renewing of ties. A rebuilding of broken bridges. A rejoicing in the prodigal come home.

Communal forgiveness happens daily, hourly, as we confess known sins and "get right" with the Father. There's a supernatural cleansing that takes place. An inner "setting free." A release from the bonds of guilt, fear, worry, anger, resentment, indifference.

Harold Hughes, at one time a senator and alcoholic, but later a committed Christian, told a touching story about attending an Alcoholics Anonymous family fellowship meeting with his daughter, Phyllis, age seven. As they waited in the foyer for the rest of the family to come downstairs, little Phyllis suddenly said, "Daddy, why do we go to these meetings? You never drank."

A choked-up Harold Hughes sat down on the steps and pulled Phyllis to his breast, gazing into her deep brown, innocent eyes. "Honey," he explained, "I did drink once. Much of it happened before you were born and I stopped drinking before you were old enough to remember."

He paused, then added, "Yes, your daddy did have a very sad drinking problem."

Phyllis hugged him tightly and said, "But you don't now, and that's all that matters."

As he held her, he savored her wisdom. *Yes, he thought, what we are today is all that matters, to a child . . . and to God.*[6]

In a sense that's the essence of both salvation and communal forgiveness. We're forgiven forever at salvation, but our communion is maintained by walking with Him today. When we stumble, we simply confess it and go on.

GETTING FORGIVENESS

There's nothing simpler in life than gaining the forgiveness offered in Christ. Merely look at your sin, recognize it as sin, agree with God that it's sin, tell Him you don't want to live that way anymore, and accept His word as final. "If we confess our sins, He is faithful and just and will forgive us our sins and purify us from all unrighteousness" (1 John 1:9). That goes for both the salvation of Christ and the communion with Christ.

It's like building a bridge. When we trust Christ, repent of sin, and begin following Him, a bridge is erected between us and Him. It can never be shattered, broken, or taken down.

However, when we sin after salvation, it's as though debris builds up on that bridge so that normal traffic can't pass. That debris is our daily sin. We remove it through confession and, if necessary, restitution to those we've sinned against. The moment we confess those sins, the debris is removed and normal traffic passes between us and Him.

As Leonardo da Vinci toiled on his painting *The Last Supper*, he had a dispute with a man and lashed him with hot words. Afterward, he returned to the painting and tried to finish the part he was working on, the face of Jesus. He couldn't get the face right. His mind rattled with the memory of his merciless words. His hand shook. Finally, he went to the man he'd wronged and asked forgiveness. The man ac-

---

[6]From a story in *Guideposts*, July 1979.

cepted his apology. When da Vinci returned to the painting, he was able to finish the face of Jesus with joy and a recognition that the job was done well.[7]

Real forgiveness can come only at the cost of real repentance and confession of sin. Gerald Ford wrote in his book *A Time to Heal* of his thoughts as he listened to President Nixon make his resignation speech in 1974. Nixon spoke of how he'd felt the need to persevere through the Watergate investigation and to complete his term of office. But Nixon realized he "no longer [had] a strong enough political base in the Congress to justify continuing that effort."

Nixon believed that with real congressional support he could see the "Constitutional process through to its conclusion. But because of the absence of such a base, there was no "longer a need for the process to be prolonged."

Nixon concluded, "To continue the fight through the months ahead for my personal vindication would almost totally absorb the time and attention of both the President and the Congress in a period when our entire focus should be on the great issues of peace abroad and prosperity without inflation at home. Therefore, I shall resign the Presidency, effective at noon tomorrow."

Ford commented, "The speech lasted 15 minutes, and at the end I was convinced that Nixon was out of touch with reality. The fact that he was linking his resignation to the loss of his Congressional base shocked me then and disturbs me still. If he'd been more contrite and asked the American people for forgiveness, he would have received a warmer response. Yet he couldn't take that final step."[8]

Asking God for forgiveness, and then supplying Him with numerous excuses, ifs, ands, or buts wins nothing but a cold response from Him. Just as Nixon's carefully worded evasion gained nothing but scorn and shame, so a lack of genuine repentance and heartfelt conviction mark a person as a fraud in the eyes of God. David was a "man after God's own heart," not because he was free of sin or because he lived a holy and godly life always—he didn't. No, he was called "the man after God's own heart" because when confronted with his sin, his

---

[7] In *Bits and Pieces*.
[8] Gerald Ford, *A Time to Heal*.

words were immediate and firm: "I have sinned." Nothing more, nothing less.

FORGIVENESS AND GOD'S PEOPLE

A pastor friend of mine uses an illustration about a boy who sinned and went up to his room. His mother asked, "What are you doing?" He answered, "I'm going up to my room to talk to God." She said, "Is it something you can tell me?" "No," the boy answered. "You'll just scold me and punish me. But God will forgive me and forget all about it."

While God's forgiveness is grand, all-encompassing, and utterly free, the hurt and pain we cause others when we sin does not go away so easily. Several of the people I interviewed no longer attend church because of the way Christians treated them following the discovery of some personal sin on their part. One woman said, "I believe in God, but I can't stand His people." Another told me, "The way some of God's so-called people act makes me not want to believe in Him at all."

Despite these episodes, I've found that most of God's people are forgiving, loving, decent folks who want to do right. But there's always one or two who kink up the works.

It remains a problem. Christians ought to be the most forgiving of all. The Lord felt so strongly about this issue, He warned us in the Sermon on the Mount, "For if you forgive men when they sin against you, your Heavenly Father will also forgive you. But if you do not forgive men their sins, Your Father will not forgive your sins" (Matt. 6:14-15). Paul reminds us repeatedly in his letters to "forgive as Christ forgave us" (see Eph. 4:31-32 and Col. 3:12-13).

Yet, we sometimes withhold from ourselves that forgiveness as a manipulative cudgel, a threat, or even out of plain revenge on ourselves. We seem to feel some sins call for a period in purgatory or a visit to "the woodshed." Yet, God makes it clear that He forgives completely and even cleanses us of the things we may have forgotten to confess (see 1 John 1:9). We are to forgive in the same way.

Still, when we sin and discover some stony Christian expects far more than "a simple confession," God provides an answer. In a sense it's the same problem David had when he had Uriah murdered. The Gentiles "blasphemed the name of God" because of his sin (see 2 Sam. 12:14). When we are accused—rightly or wrongly—Peter counsels us to "show by our good behavior" that we're truly His (see 1 Peter 2:12 and 3:16).

There's the story of the two brothers who were sheep thieves. When caught, both were branded with the letters "ST" on their necks so all would know of their crimes. One brother, ashamed and bitter, skulked throughout the world, reclusive and alone. The other, though, resolved to live right ever after. He proved himself a worthy subject and did good deeds the rest of his life. Years later, a child asked his father why the man had "ST" on his neck. The father replied, "I forget what it stood for originally, but folks say now that it means 'saint.' "

I like what Dr. Lewis Sperry Chafer told a church leader who committed adultery several times during his ministry. The leader complained, "God forgave me. Why don't people forgive me?" He believed he should be back preaching now that he'd repented of his sin. Chafer answered, "God knows your heart, but the people do not."

There is something to be said for God's people forgiving us in the expectation of seeing some real results in our lives. John the Baptist told the Pharisees who came to him for baptism to "produce fruit in keeping with repentance" (Matt. 3:8). Paul told Agrippa, "To the Gentiles . . . I preached that they should repent and turn to God and prove their repentance by their deeds" (Acts 26:20). It's the same idea James promoted when he wrote, "Show me your faith without deeds, and I will show you my faith by what I do" (James 2:18). We are to forgive a man who repents seventy times seven times (really infinitely), but not a man who refuses to repent, or who repents falsely with no effort at real change. If you've sinned and confessed it but find some Christians skeptical, don't fret. Just live right and they will soon become convinced you're for real.

GOD'S WAY OF FORGIVENESS

How does God forgive us when we give in to temptation? There's a story about a man who has sinned the same sin so many times, he reels with shame. He comes to God one more time hoping and praying that somehow God will find it in His heart to give him one last chance. He says, "Lord, I'm so ashamed. I've done this sin over and over. I swear I'll never do it again. Please forgive me."

A voice from heaven shakes the man to his bones. "Yes, I will forgive you. The sin is completely forgotten. You are free to begin again with a clean slate."

The man is jubilant. He kicks his feet, cries, "Hallelujah!" and thanks God over and over. He knows this time he's beaten it. It's over. He'll never do it again. But then that night the juices start flowing and in moments he's sinned before he's thought about it.

He's so ashamed he can't pray. He feels he's let God down one too many times. There's no way he can go to Him. He tells himself just to give it up, he's no Christian, he should forget the whole thing. But his conscience convicts him, so he finally crawls to his bed and moans, "Lord, I'm so ashamed. I don't even have the right to talk to You. I did it again."

The august voice speaks. "What did you do?"

He chokes out the words. "That sin, the one I confessed to You this morning."

There's a long pause. He knows God must be looking at the books, perhaps thinking of an apt punishment. But then the voice says, "Sorry. There's no record of any sin. And I certainly don't remember one. So what did you want to discuss?"[9]

When we confess our sins to God, He forgives us completely, eternally, with no mention of it ever again. That's real forgiveness, the kind worth gaining in Christ.

FRIENDS

I've referred in this chapter several times to Watergate and President Nixon. Strangely, it seemed that they were appropriate illustrations. I don't mean to single him out as some awful sinner. But one other story has always stuck with me about those terrible days. In 1979, having established himself

---

[9]Paraphrased from Tim Stafford and Philip Yancey, *Unhappy Secrets of the Christian Life* (Grand Rapids, Mich.: Zondervan, 1979), p. 60.

as a minister and evangelist in a prison ministry, Chuck Colson addressed a college audience that was obviously hostile. Colson fielded a number of questions about Watergate. But finally, one student stood and angrily confronted him about his relationship with former President Nixon. There was a bitter silence and Colson hesitated at the microphone. Then with quiet but firm tones, Colson responded, "Richard Nixon is my friend."

One might have expected an eruption of angry and hot words. Instead, the audience applauded.[10]

I suspect that Jesus would say the same thing about us.

---

[10]From an article by R.C. Sproul in *Tabletalk*, August 1979.

BATTLE'S END

THE STRANGENESS OF GOD'S WAYS

CHAPTER 18

God works in strange ways."

So goes a famous saying. Yet it's true. God does work in strange ways. In fact, God's ways are downright incredible.

God could have created a universe where everyone obeyed Him instantly, always and completely, without argument, excuse, or failure. He might have created a world where men and women lived always and only in perfect harmony with Him and with one another. He could have easily begun the world without a problem and kept things going forever without an interference.

But God didn't do it that way. Instead, He created a world . . .

. . . in which sin and rebellion were possible, probable, and even profitable for those who might commit it.

. . . in which His Son would have to die—something He knew before He even created it.

. . . in which those who call themselves His people would

often be regarded as the dregs of society.

... where His plan would look like a complete failure right up until the very end.

... in which most of mankind would reject Him.

... in which sin, insubordination, rebellion, and transgression would be preferable to holiness in the eyes of most of its inhabitants.

... where He would allow the devil to roam far and free in tempting and destroying His subjects.

Could there have been a more foolish and pain-ridden act? Many would say, "No. The divine experiment is a colossal failure, a hopeless debacle. God should go back to the drawing board."

But perhaps there was and is no other way. Perhaps this is the only way God can create beings in His image who can make moral choices. Perhaps fashioning creatures with a genuine right to choose between good and evil carries with it great risk, even for God. Perhaps to arrive at a perfect, unified, and holy universe, we must go through the debacle of Satan's rebellion, the sin of Planet Earth and either atonement or hell.

Truly, God's "thoughts are not our thoughts, and His ways are not our ways." Few if any of us would have chosen this route. But we are not in a position to choose. He decided the limits, places, times, things, and people. We decide only if we will follow Him, or the world, flesh, and devil.

But God's ways remain strange. Consider for a moment some of the almost aggravating truths that permeate the Bible.

"To be weak is to be strong." Paul said in 2 Corinthians 12:9-10 that when God refused to remove a thorn in his flesh, he discovered God's grace was sufficient, for "[His] power is made perfect in weakness." Paul's conclusion: "I will boast ... about my weaknesses, so that Christ's power may rest on me." What did Paul mean? When we come to the end of ourselves, after we have tried and failed repeatedly on our own, only then do we look to Him. Our weakness drives us to Him. And in Him we find hope and genuine spiritual power.

This principle holds true in the problem of temptation.

Only when we realize we can't do it on our own will we move in His direction. Then He begins giving us the resources to overcome.

"Bad can be used for good." Romans 8:28 must be the life verse of everyone who is tempted: "We know that in all things God works for the good of those who love Him, who have been called according to His purpose." Sins, failures, errors, mistakes, transgressions, iniquities, "horrors beyond redemption"—whatever you want to call them—somehow God can transform that wrongdoing so that something good emerges in the end. No sinner need fear that his life has become worthless or useless. Nothing he does can checkmate, stalemate, or cancel the power of God. There are consequences of sin. We may be impaired because of a failure. But we are never considered despicable. We can count on God's goodness and power to turn even the worst measures for good.

"We get right by admitting we are wrong." Jesus said, "If you do not believe I am the One I claim to be, you will indeed die in your sins" (John 8:24). It's like what C.S. Lewis' Spirit says in *The Great Divorce.* "That's what we all find when we reach this country. We've all been wrong! That's the great joke. There's no need to go on pretending one was right! After that we begin living."[1]

True freedom comes through an admission: "I'm a sinner. I'm wrong. I've blown it. There can be no recovery apart from You." When we come to that place, we are truly set free. We no longer have to pretend. No more playing games. No more making excuses and hiding and hoping no one knows the truth. Now we can live, because we know the truth about ourselves is known by Him who knows all and He has forgiven us.

"We find life by losing it." Jesus said, "Whoever finds his life shall lose it, and whoever loses his life for My sake will find it" (Matt. 10:39). He meant that if we hold onto life in this world as if that were all that matters, in the end we'll lose it. We will die and go to hell. But if we give up, submit ourselves to Him, and give Him our hearts, our souls, our lives for His use, then in the end we gain life eternal.

---

[1]C.S. Lewis, *The Great Divorce* (Wheaton, Ill.: Christianity Today, 1969), p. 172.

Again, as we face temptation, we find true life—joy, peace, hope, love, kindness, goodness, self-control—only by giving up the old ways, the old self, the old mind-sets and attitudes. Only as we lose ourselves in service and love for Him do we begin to conquer ourselves.

"Without God, nothing has value; with God, everything has infinite value." Jesus said of the rich fool, "This very night your life will be demanded from you. Then who will get what you have prepared for yourself?" (Luke 12:20) His life and all he had became worthless—to him and everyone else. Why? Because he left out God. Jesus said, "Apart from Me you can do nothing" (John 15:5).

It doesn't matter what we do in life if we live without God. It's all worthless, foolishness, vanity, striving after wind. Like Solomon expressed in Ecclesiastes, we can do little more than hate our lives.

But with God, everything comes into focus. People have new value. Words, acts, thoughts suddenly glitter with the glow of eternity. Every little deed counts before heaven. Nothing is lost. Nothing is forgotten. Life is not the "tale told by an idiot," as Macbeth said, "full of sound and fury, signifying nothing." Rather, it's the "all time adventure story authored by God, full of sound, lights, and action, signifying everything."

We're in a war, but the war has already been won. Jesus saw Satan plummet from heaven like lightning (Luke 10:18). He who is in us is greater than he who is in the world (1 John 4:4). And we are to "take courage" because Christ has "overcome the world" (John 16:33).

As I said in the first chapter, we're in a war. But there's one great difference in this war: it's already been won. The conclusion has not only been decided; it's been reached. Christ dealt Satan, the world, and the flesh their death blows at the cross. The battle was over then. Finis. Done. Tetelestai. The end.

You might gaze over the battlefield of your life and think, "It's been won? Ha! Then I must have been on the losing side."

It may look that way to you, but then you're not looking at it through the lenses of Scripture. You don't have to beat

Satan; all you must do is "stand firm." You don't have to overcome the world; all you must do is "hold fast." You needn't think you have to obliterate the flesh; all you need do is "be strong and courageous."

That's all. Just don't give up. Just hang in there. Just tough it out. Christ's day is coming.

One of the most thrilling scenes in all the movies I've ever seen occurs in the first *Rocky* movie. Sylvester Stallone is Rocky Balboa, the Italian Stallion. He's the loser who's been given a crack at the heavyweight championship of the world. Rocky is a true nobody. He struggles from being afraid, out of shape. He's a hopeless guinea pig in a big promotion campaign that his opponent, Apollo Creed, is pushing. Rocky just hopes he can hang in there for fifteen rounds. Now it's the night before the bout, which is scheduled for New Year's Eve. Rocky's done all he can to prepare. He's worked out, trained, flattened his stomach to the hardness of rock. He's run his miles, thrown his shots, given his all.

But that night he goes over to the Philadelphia Spectrum where the match will be held. He gazes around at the huge posters of Creed and himself hanging from the ceiling. He sees the glitter and the glory. And deep down he knows he's so far out of his league, so far removed from all he's ever done, he feels like a high school footballer going to the Super Bowl. There's no way he can win.

He goes home to his girlfriend Adrienne, depressed and fearful. But as he lays on the bed, thinking, hoping against hope, the realization comes to him. He says to her: "I can't do it."

"What?" Adrienne asks, brushing the sleep out of her eyes.

"I can't beat him."

"Apollo?"

"Yeah." Rocky looks tired, disheveled, half-beaten already. "I been out there walkin' around, thinkin'. I mean, who am I kiddin'? I ain't even in the guy's league."

Adrienne sits up, touches his massive shoulder. "What are we going to do?"

"I don't know."

"But you worked so hard."

"Yeah, but it don't matter, cause I was nobody before."

"Don't say that."

Rocky shakes his head. "Come on, Adrienne, it's true. I was nobody." The words are hard and cruel, tinged almost with despair.

Then: "But it really don't matter if I lose this fight. It really don't matter if this guy opens my head either. Cause all that I really want to do is go the distance."

There's another long pause and Rocky says in his thick accent: "Nobody's ever gone the distance with Creed. And if I can go that distance—if that bell rings and I'm still standin' "—the voice is heavy with emotion now, the plaintive cry of a hopeless man finding real hope—"then I'm gonna know for the first time in my life—see—that I weren't just another bum from the neighborhood."

Everytime I see that movie, everytime I hear Rocky say those words, I think of another bell, another time, another place—that last trumpet when we are caught up to meet Christ in the air, when we will all face Him for the first time. It's then that I pray to God I'm still standing, still kicking, still dealing blows to the enemy. I know I'm not in the same league as the devil. I know if it's just me and him, it's over. But God doesn't expect us to go it alone. All He wants is that we keep on our feet, stand firm, and not give in. He'll be there with us. Always. Right to the end. All He wants us to do is go the distance. "Fight the good fight. Finish the race."

That's all I want to do. What about you?